Discover the *ADVENTURE* of You

A Practical Workbook to Unlock Your Authentic Self, Empower Your Mind, Nourish Your Body, and Ignite Your Soul!

CHRISTINE D ROSS

BALBOA.PRESS
A DIVISION OF HAY HOUSE

Balboa Press books may be ordered through booksellers or by contacting:

Balboa Press
A Division of Hay House
1663 Liberty Drive
Bloomington, IN 47403
www.balboapress.com
844-682-1282

Print information available on the last page.

ISBN: 979-8-7652-4551-4 (sc)
ISBN: 979-8-7652-4553-8 (hc)
ISBN: 979-8-7652-4552-1 (e)

Library of Congress Control Number: 2023917774

Balboa Press rev. date: 11/14/2023

To Travis, my unconditional source of love, strength, and support. Your belief in me has been the guiding light that has illuminated my path, and your unwavering support has given me the courage to share my insights with the world. Thank you for standing by my side through every step of our journey, encouraging me, and being a listening ear as I process my thoughts into words. This book is dedicated to you, my husband, best friend, confidant, and greatest inspiration.

I would also like to express my deepest gratitude to my children, who have brought immeasurable joy, love, and inspiration into my life. You are my greatest teachers and soulmates, and witnessing your growth and development has enriched my journey in ways I never thought possible. I am grateful for the lessons you have taught me about love, resilience, and the beauty of embracing life's adventures.

In addition, I extend my appreciation to the incredible teachers who have graced my life with wisdom and knowledge and to all the countless individuals who have touched my life, directly or indirectly. Each interaction, conversation, and shared experience has left an indelible mark on my journey. Your stories, experiences, and wisdom have ignited a fire within me to delve deeper, grow, and embrace the essence of our existence. Thank you for opening your life, sharing your knowledge, and participating in my life journey.

From the depths of my heart, I express my sincerest gratitude to each of you for being a source of inspiration, growth, and connection. Your presence and influence have played a vital role in shaping my adventure. With profound appreciation, I acknowledge the impact you have had on my life and the deep gratitude I feel for the role you have played.

Discover the Adventure of You

Are you prepared to venture into the depths of your being, Where the secrets of self-discovery lie waiting to be revealed? Unleash the dormant power within, radiant and bright, To shape a life of health, joy, and vibrant light.

Embark on this journey, a sacred quest, Where healing waters soothe the wounded soul's unrest. With each step, gain awareness of thoughts and ways, Transforming habits, nurturing relationships, throughout the days.

In the pages of this book, a guide for your ascent, Uncover your true self, divine and magnificent. An adventure unfolds, a tapestry unfurls, Of personal growth and transformation, a story of precious pearls.

Embrace the chapters, as petals unfurling, Unveiling the depths, where authenticity is swirling. Discover the treasures, the gems deep within, As you forge a path to wholeness and begin.

So with an open heart and mind, take this leap, Embrace the journey, let your soul's whispers seep. For within these words lies the essence of you, A fulfilling adventure, a life rich and true.

CONTENTS

This book is intended as a self-help guide for individuals seeking personal growth and development. It is important to note that this book does not replace professional medical advice, therapy, or treatment. If you are experiencing severe emotional distress, struggling with mental health issues, or having thoughts of suicide, it is crucial to seek immediate medical help or consult a qualified healthcare professional. The exercises and practices in this workbook are designed to promote well-being and self-discovery. Still, they should be approached with care and in consideration of your individual needs and circumstances.

Throughout this book, I have shared my own authentic stories and experiences to illustrate the power of transformation and personal growth. These stories are based on my personal journey, and the names and identifying details have not been changed. However, regarding the stories involving my clients, I have taken great care to protect their privacy. Names and identifying information have been altered to ensure anonymity, and the stories are a composite of experiences from multiple clients to illustrate common themes of growth and healing. I value the trust and confidentiality of all individuals involved, and their privacy remains paramount.

Welcome to "Discover the Adventure of You: A Practical Workbook to Unlock Your Authentic Self, Empower Your Mind, Nourish Your Body, and Ignite Your Soul"! This workbook is designed to be a companion on your personal journey of self-exploration and growth. Here are a few tips to help you navigate this workbook effectively:

1. **Take your time:** This workbook is meant to be worked through at your own pace. You can choose to go through it page by page, following the order of the chapters, or feel free to jump to different chapters that resonate with you at various stages of your journey.
2. **Trust the process:** Some exercises or prompts may seem similar or repetitive, but trust that each one serves a unique purpose in your self-discovery and growth. Sometimes revisiting or approaching

a topic from a different angle can help unleash new insights and perspectives.

3. **Create a supportive environment:** Find a quiet and comfortable space where you can focus and reflect without distractions. Consider using a journal or notebook to record your thoughts, reflections, and insights throughout the workbook.
4. **Be kind to yourself:** Remember that this workbook is about self-discovery and personal growth. Approach the exercises with an open mind and a compassionate attitude toward yourself. Embrace the journey and allow yourself to learn and grow along the way.
5. **Adapt to your needs:** Feel free to adapt the exercises and practices to suit your preferences and needs. Modify them as necessary to make them more meaningful and relevant to your unique circumstances.

Please remember that this workbook is a tool to support your personal development but is not a substitute for professional help or therapy. If you encounter any challenges or feel overwhelmed during the process, it is essential to reach out to qualified professionals who can provide the necessary support and guidance.

You are the author of your own story, and this workbook, "Discover the Adventure of You," is here to inspire and assist you on this remarkable journey of self-exploration. Embrace the adventure and trust in the process as you uncover the depths of who you truly are. Allow yourself to fully engage with the exercises, reflect on your insights, and take meaningful action towards creating a happy, healthy, and fulfilling life. Your journey of self-discovery starts now.

Enjoy the adventure!

INTRODUCTION

Embarking on a Transformative Journey

Hey there, fellow human! It's time to get unstuck and release all that trauma and emotional baggage you've been carrying around. I understand how overwhelming life can be and the challenges we face in navigating through it. But fear not, because together, we can overcome anything that comes our way.

Think of yourself as a vehicle. On this adventure of life, we sometimes cruise effortlessly, enjoying the picturesque views and the wind in our hair. But, like any vehicle, there are moments when we might stall, get a flat tire, or even need an engine overhaul. And just as a car requires regular maintenance to keep it running smoothly, we too require constant care and attention to ensure we're operating at our best. While vehicles come with manuals detailing their care, we're often left trying to navigate the complexities of our own existence without a guide.

Occasionally, we find ourselves on autopilot, not actively deciding our path but merely reacting to the world around us. Ask yourself—who turned on this autopilot? Did you set the current destination, or are you unwittingly following a course charted by someone else's expectations, societal norms, or past traumas? Remember, you are in the driver's seat. You have the power to set your own course, find your true purpose, and map out the most fulfilling route to your destination.

Taking care of ourselves doesn't merely end with the physical—eating nutritious food and staying active. Our mental well-being is equally, if not more, crucial. A car may have a pristine exterior, but accidents can happen if the driver behind the wheel is distracted or overwhelmed. Similarly, when we're bombarded with emotions, stress, and the chaos of daily life, our mental fog can lead us to make decisions that aren't aligned with our true selves, leaving us feeling drained and distant.

But here's the silver lining—just as you have the power to veer off course, you also have the power to get back on track. Shift from autopilot to manual to reignite your passion, purpose, and zest for life. Live life consciously, carry out regular "self-checks," and ensure you're aligned with your goals and values.

Change, although daunting, is the bridge between stagnation and growth. Ask yourself —do you want to relive the same patterns year after year, feeling like you're stuck in a time loop? Or would you rather embrace each moment filled with adventures, learning, and unparalleled experiences?

Remember, while the road of life has its twists, turns, and occasional potholes, you have the map, the steering wheel, and the keys. The choice, as always, is yours. It's time to turn off the autopilot, take the wheel, and drive toward your destined greatness.

Are you ready for an overall wellness tune-up? Please allow me to assist you.

Hi, I'm Christine D Ross. Envision me as your personal wellness mechanic. My expertise lies not in machinery but in the intricate workings of the human mind and body. I'm here to guide you toward realizing and achieving the best version of yourself. Armed with credentials as an NCCA board-certified Health and Wellness Coach, Life/empowerment Coach, and Fitness Nutrition Specialist, I've immersed myself in the intricate world of health and wellness. My commitment and passion are not just reflections of my formal education but are deeply rooted in personal experiences—notably, a profound journey of resilience as I faced and overcame the challenges of cancer.

Drawing from these experiences, I've developed powerful tools and strategies that have the potential to recalibrate and rejuvenate your life, aligning it with wellness, purpose, and joy. Are you prepared to embrace change, shift gears, and charge ahead on a path that promises health, happiness, and fulfillment? Then grab onto the steering wheel and buckle up. Together, we're going on a transformative journey, and I promise you, it will be a wild ride!

In this book, I'll be your guide as we uncover the tools and strategies that have helped me and my clients create healthy habits, overcome obstacles, and live a life filled with purpose and joy. Trust me—if I can do it, so can you!

Maybe you feel stuck and don't know where to turn, or perhaps you've received one of life's "wake-up calls" and are ready to heal and possibly reverse illness. Whatever your starting point, I'm here to help you take control of your thoughts and optimize your health to feel more energized with a clear mind and freedom in your body. Plus, this book is a perfect fit if you're passionate about living a lifestyle that supports healing our earth.

Get ready to hit the road to success! Together, we'll learn how to stay motivated, set and achieve goals, nourish our mind, body, and spirit, cultivate healthy relationships, and much more. Think of this book as your own personal GPS, casually guiding you through the twists and turns of life.

Now, I know what you're thinking: "Another wellness book? Really?" But hear me out. This isn't your average preachy, holier-than-thou stuffy health manual. Instead, this is a practical, down-to-earth workbook designed to help you unlock your full potential and create a life that radiates from the inside out. We'll cry and have some laughs and fun along the way because let's be real—if we're not enjoying the ride, what's the point?

So buckle up, and let's hit the road to success. Each day allow yourself free time for journaling, affirmations, and mindfulness. Take the time needed to contemplate each question, create goals, and action plans. Together, we'll get rid of all that old worn-out baggage, avoid those pesky potholes, make some positive changes, and cruise down the highway of life with ease. Get ready to transform into a brand-new, souped-up version of yourself. It's time to put the pedal to the metal and discover the adventure of you!

1

Daily Tools for Motivation

Motivation, not success, serves as the key to achieving one's goals. When we are motivated, success naturally follows.

Igniting Your Inner Drive

Let's face it—staying motivated can be trickier than finding a needle in a haystack. But fear not, my fellow friend! I have some tips and tricks that will keep you motivated and feel like a superhero in no time. Ironically, the best way to stay motivated comes from doing it. So the more you "do" think positive thoughts, "do" eat healthily, and "do" exercise, the better you will feel, and soon, feeling good will become your motivation.

It's important to note that each of these tools for motivation will be explored in much greater detail in the following chapters. Each topic will be examined thoroughly, providing you with the guidance and support you need to uncover your deepest motivations. From affirmations and gratitude exercises to self-reflection and goal-setting techniques, these tools will become your trusted allies on your path to personal fulfillment.

1. Daily **affirmations and gratitude** practice. You know what they say: "An attitude of gratitude brings forth a magnitude of goodness." So take a few minutes each day to be grateful for what is working in your body and life. And while you're at it, write down at least nine things you're thankful for. It's like counting sheep, but instead of falling asleep, you'll be waking up to the good things in life.

2. **Discover your bottom line *why***. Write it and say it out loud several times a day if necessary. Paste it on the fridge, your mirror, or anywhere. You deserve to have a constant reminder of why you are determined to create this lifestyle change.
3. **Visualize**. Visualize the life you want to live. Spend at least five minutes daily putting your powerful mind to work. Picture yourself succeeding in even the smallest of goals. Create a mental picture of yourself accomplishing tasks and living a healthy life. Trust me: your mind is powerful, and visualizing your success can increase your chances of achieving it.
4. **Practice mindful eating**. You're more likely to eat nourishing foods and much less likely to overeat when you eat mindfully. When we eat mindfully, we are more aware of how our food makes us feel and how it affects our bodies, which can lead to making healthier choices. Plus, who doesn't love feeling like a food critic, taking the time to really taste and appreciate every bite?
5. **Exercise daily**, even if it's just for fifteen minutes of walking and some stretching. Think of it as a mini-disco party for your brain. When you work up a sweat, your body releases endorphins—the "happy hormones"—that make you feel like you just won the lottery (or at least like you're not stuck in traffic anymore). Plus, exercise is a terrific way to meet new people and bond over the mutual pain of burpees and squats. Who knows, maybe you'll even find your new BFF while doing lunges.
6. **Develop a healthy bedtime ritual**. Let's face it—without a good night's sleep, we're basically zombies stumbling through the day. But with a healthy bedtime routine, you can transform from a groggy mess to a motivated machine! By shutting off electronics, taking a warm bath, and reading an enjoyable book, you're telling your body, "Hey, it's time to chill out and get some serious shuteye."

And when you wake up feeling energized and ready to conquer the world, you'll know that your bedtime routine is the real MVP.

7. **Think big**. Thinking big is motivating because it allows you to see the potential of what you can achieve beyond your current circumstances. When you think big, you're not limiting yourself to small goals that may not be challenging enough or may not make a significant impact on your life and the world around you. Instead, you're reaching for the stars and dreaming of what's possible, giving you a sense of purpose, excitement, and motivation to take action toward your goals. Why settle for small dreams when you can aim for the stars (while keeping your feet on the ground, of course)?
8. **Create goals and put them into action**. Checking items off a to-do list feels like a victory parade in your brain! It's like your brain is saying, "Yeah, baby, we did it!" Accomplishing your goals gives you that sweet satisfaction that only comes from knowing you nailed it. And let's not forget the additional motivation that comes from showing off your list to anyone who will listen so you can bask in their admiration and praise.
9. **Take small steps**. Taking small steps motivates us to see progress and feel a sense of accomplishment along the way. It's like climbing a mountain—you don't start at the top; you take one step at a time. By breaking down our goals into smaller, manageable tasks, we can avoid feeling overwhelmed and stay motivated as we achieve our bigger goals. Plus, completing each small step can give us a little confidence boost and make us feel like we're on the right track.
10. **Stay Committed**. When you commit, you are essentially making a promise to yourself to follow through on your intentions. And let's be real—breaking promises to yourself is a surefire way to make you feel like a total flake. So by staying committed, you

maintain your integrity and build self-trust, which can increase your motivation and drive to succeed. Plus, staying motivated is much easier when you're not constantly second-guessing your commitment. "If it's to be, it's up to me and my committed action." Say your commitment statement at least three times in a row, three times a day.

11. **Be accountable**. It's not all rainbows and unicorns. Being accountable for your thoughts, feelings, and actions is always best. And when something doesn't work for you, learn from it, and look for other ways to succeed. Different options can give you a new perspective and more energy.
12. **Harness the power of positivity**. The belief that you can accomplish something is essential to your ability to do it. Being positive can help us stay motivated because it allows us to see opportunities instead of obstacles. When we have a positive mindset, we are more likely to believe in ourselves and our abilities, giving us the confidence to take on challenges and pursue our goals. Plus, being negative all the time is plain exhausting. Who wants to be a constant Debbie Downer when you could be an Optimistic Oliver?
13. **Figure out your triggers**. Knowing your triggers can motivate you to proactively plan how to deal with potential roadblocks and prevent them from derailing your progress. It's like having a secret weapon in your back pocket—you can anticipate the obstacles and devise strategies to overcome them. Plus, being able to say, "I know my weaknesses, and I've got this," can be a huge confidence booster!
14. **Restrict your distractions**. Do your best to keep toxic food and people out of your life that tempt you to make choices that aren't in line with your desired lifestyle. When you are easily distracted, you may lose sight of what you're trying to achieve

and waste time and effort on things that don't matter. Plus, there's nothing more satisfying than the feeling of accomplishment when you've successfully resisted the temptation to procrastinate or get sidetracked by something else. It's like giving yourself a mental high-five and saying, "Way to go, me! I'm crushing it!"

15. **Remain in the zone**. Create the perfect environment that supports your goals and assists you in making good, healthy choices. It's like building your own personal motivational fortress. Staying "in the zone" can be like living in your own productive little bubble. It's like wearing noise-canceling headphones but for distractions. And who wouldn't want to be in a state of flow where the only thing you're flowing with is productivity and success? It's like being a superhero, but instead of fighting crime, you're conquering your goals and achieving your dreams!
16. **Have fun!** Because if it's not fun, you won't stick with it. So create an environment that supports your goals and aids you in making good, healthy choices. And don't forget to laugh, smile, and enjoy the journey. Because life is too short not to have fun along the way.
17. **Honor and celebrate your achievements**. Celebrating achievements can be incredibly motivating because it helps to reinforce the positive behavior that led to the accomplishment. By recognizing and celebrating our successes, we feel a sense of pride and accomplishment that can fuel us to continue working toward our goals. Additionally, celebrating achievements can provide a much-needed break from the daily grind and help us appreciate our progress so far. And who doesn't enjoy a good celebration?

Remember that whether you think you can or think you can't, you're right. So harness the power of positivity, restrict your distractions, and remain in the zone. And if all else fails, just keep on keepin' on, my friend. You got this!

Daily Affirmations and Gratitude Practices

Harness the power within with daily affirmations and a gratitude practice! In the following pages, you will find a treasure trove of affirmations and gratitude prompts to uplift and inspire you on your journey. So get ready to embark on an eight-week adventure of self-discovery and growth.

Grab a journal or some extra sheets of paper to fully immerse yourself in this practice. Each week, you will find a set of affirmations and gratitude prompts tailored to enhance specific aspects of your life. Feel free to write them down, allowing the words to flow from your heart onto the pages. This act of writing solidifies your commitment to the practice and amplifies its impact.

As you begin each week, take a moment to ground yourself in the present moment. Breathe deeply and set your intention for the week ahead. Then delve into the affirmations provided for that week. Read them aloud, let the words resonate within you, and embrace the positive energy they carry. Repeat them daily, allowing them to infuse your thoughts, beliefs, and actions with empowerment and positivity.

You will find space to reflect and express your gratitude in writing alongside the affirmations. This simple act of acknowledging and savoring the blessings in your life has the power to shift your perspective and attract more positivity.

At the end of each week, take a moment to reflect on your experiences, insights, and growth. Use the additional pages provided for additional affirmations that resonate with you. This space is yours to explore, create, and make the practice your own.

Remember that consistency is key in harnessing the full potential of this practice. Commit to dedicating a few moments each day to affirmations and gratitude. Let them become your daily companions, guiding you toward a life filled with joy, abundance, and fulfillment.

So grab your journal or some sheets of paper, and let's embark on this transformative journey of daily affirmations and gratitude. Embrace the process, infuse it with your unique essence, and watch as the seeds of positivity and appreciation blossom within you.

Daily Affirmation and Gratitude Process

Week One, Date: _____

Daily Statement: ***I consciously make choices that support healing myself and the earth.***

1. Read the daily statement aloud nine times.
2. Write the daily statement three times.

____

____

____

____

____

3. Read the daily statement three more times out loud.
4. Close your eyes and take nine deep breaths in. Really feel the energy of this statement.
5. Sit in silence and relax for a few minutes.
6. List nine things for which you are grateful.

I am grateful for

____

____

____

____

____

Daily Affirmation and Gratitude Process

Week Two, Date: ____________

Daily Statement: ***I Love myself, my body, and everything I do.***

1. Read the daily statement aloud nine times.
2. Write the daily statement three times.

____

____

____

____

____

3. Read the daily statement three more times out loud.
4. Close your eyes and take nine deep breaths in. Really feel the energy of this statement.
5. Sit in silence and relax for a few minutes.
6. List nine things for which you are grateful.

I am grateful for

____

____

____

____

____

Daily Affirmation and Gratitude Process

Week Three, Date: ____________

Daily Statement: ***I release all worry, doubt, fears, and attachment to ____________. All good things come to me now.***

1. Read the daily statement aloud nine times.
2. Write the daily statement three times.

____

____

____

____

____

3. Read the daily statement three more times out loud.
4. Close your eyes and take nine deep breaths in. Really feel the energy of this statement.
5. Sit in silence and relax for a few minutes.
6. List nine things for which you are grateful.

I am grateful for

____

____

____

____

____

Daily Affirmation and Gratitude Process

Week Four, Date: ____________

Daily Statement: ***I am a beautiful person who deserves happiness, health, and peace.***

1. Read the daily statement aloud nine times.
2. Write the daily statement three times.

____

____

____

____

____

3. Read the daily statement three more times out loud.
4. Close your eyes and take nine deep breaths in. Really feel the energy of this statement.
5. Sit in silence and relax for a few minutes.
6. List nine things for which you are grateful.

I am grateful for

____

____

____

____

____

Daily Affirmation and Gratitude Process

Week Five, Date: ___________

Daily Statement: ***I lovingly listen to my body and know how to nourish and support it in staying healthy.***

1. Read the daily statement aloud nine times.
2. Write the daily statement three times.

____

____

____

____

____

3. Read the daily statement three more times out loud.
4. Close your eyes and take nine deep breaths in. Really feel the energy of this statement.
5. Sit in silence and relax for a few minutes.
6. List nine things for which you are grateful.

I am grateful for

____

____

____

____

____

Daily Affirmation and Gratitude Process

Week Six, Date: ____________

Daily Statement: ***I am making healthy eating, exercise, and lifestyle habits I will have for the rest of my life.***

1. Read the daily statement aloud nine times.
2. Write the daily statement three times.

____

____

____

____

____

3. Read the daily statement three more times out loud.
4. Close your eyes and take nine deep breaths in. Really feel the energy of this statement.
5. Sit in silence and relax for a few minutes.
6. List nine things for which you are grateful.

I am grateful for

____

____

____

____

____

Daily Affirmation and Gratitude Process

Week Seven, Date: ____________

Daily Statement: ***I consciously create mental and emotional balance, helping my body's natural healing mechanisms to function.***

1. Read the daily statement aloud nine times.
2. Write the daily statement three times.

____

____

____

____

____

3. Read the daily statement three more times out loud.
4. Close your eyes and take nine deep breaths in. Really feel the energy of this statement.
5. Sit in silence and relax for a few minutes.
6. List nine things for which you are grateful.

I am grateful for

____

____

____

____

____

Daily Affirmation and Gratitude Process

Week Eight, Date: ______________

Daily Statement: ***I am making choices today that my future self will thank me for.***

1. Read the daily statement aloud nine times.
2. Write the daily statement three times.

____

____

____

____

____

3. Read the daily statement three more times out loud.
4. Close your eyes and take nine deep breaths in. Really feel the energy of this statement.
5. Sit in silence and relax for a few minutes.
6. List nine things for which you are grateful.

I am grateful for

____

____

____

____

____

Daily Affirmation and Gratitude Process

Date: ____________

Daily Statement: ____

____.

1. Read the daily statement aloud nine times.
2. Write the daily statement three times.

____

____

____

____

____

3. Read the daily statement three more times out loud.
4. Close your eyes and take nine deep breaths in. Really feel the energy of this statement.
5. Sit in silence and relax for a few minutes.
6. List nine things for which you are grateful.

I am grateful for

____

____

____

____

____

Daily Affirmation and Gratitude Process

Date: ____________

Daily Statement:____

____.

1. Read the daily statement aloud nine times.
2. Write the daily statement three times.

____

____

____

____

____

3. Read the daily statement three more times out loud.
4. Close your eyes and take nine deep breaths in. Really feel the energy of this statement.
5. Sit in silence and relax for a few minutes.
6. List nine things for which you are grateful.

I am grateful for

____

____

____

____

____

Daily Affirmation and Gratitude Process

Date: ______________

Daily Statement: ____

____.

1. Read the daily statement aloud nine times.
2. Write the daily statement three times.

____

____

____

____

____

3. Read the daily statement three more times out loud.
4. Close your eyes and take nine deep breaths in. Really feel the energy of this statement.
5. Sit in silence and relax for a few minutes.
6. List nine things for which you are grateful.

I am grateful for

____

____

____

____

____

2

Navigating Wake-Up Calls

A sudden wake-up call can shake us out of our familiar routines, ultimately propelling us to discover our greatest potential.

Rise, Reflect, and Redirect

Hey friend! Have you ever had a "wake-up call" that jolted you out of your routine and made you re-evaluate your life? Many of my clients have, and I know I sure have! First, let me tell you about a client friend of mine that I will call Mary to protect her identity.

Throughout her life, Mary was taught to be, speak, and act like someone else. Forever being judged and told she wasn't good enough, she carried the scars of past abuse, hiding her true self behind walls of self-doubt. Moreover, her emotional struggles manifested as physical weight, and she found herself trapped in an unhealthy cycle.

On a tranquil Hawaiian beach, everything changed. Imagine a stunning Hawaiian day, the sun casting a warm glow, the rhythmic waves crashing against the shore, and Mary, feeling trapped in a fortress of suppressed traumas and a smile that conceals her true feelings. She lay stuck in the weight of her past burdens, feeling depressed, heavy, and unmotivated. It's like she's mired in quicksand, but instead of dirt, it's emotions dragging her down.

As Mary lay there, gazing at the ocean's vastness, she noticed children playing joyously in the waves. Their carefree laughter and uninhibited spirit stir something within her—memories of the person she was before the world told her who to be. She yearned to find that person again, who could sing aloud, dance like no one was watching, and be as free as the children on the beach.

The children's laughter and uninhibited spirit were a poignant wake-up call for Mary. At that moment, she realized that life had become a series of routines, and she had lost touch with her authentic essence. She felt an inner calling to unleash herself from the shackles of the past and embark on a transformative journey of self-discovery.

With this newfound awareness, Mary set an intention to heal the wounds of her past, knowing that in doing so, she would also release the heavy physical weight she carried. The wake-up call on that Hawaiian beach had planted a seed of change within her, and she knew she couldn't ignore it any longer.

Sometimes, all it takes is a wake-up call to realize that you need to make a change. Seeing the children's carefree spirit made Mary realize that she needed to break down the walls of her fortress. This moment of awakening marked the beginning of a remarkable journey as she embraced the adventure of unlocking her true self, seeking authenticity, and pursuing a life filled with purpose, joy, and boundless possibilities.

Disclaimer Note: The client story presented above is a fictionalized composite of experiences from multiple clients I have worked with. Names, identifying details, and specific circumstances have been changed to protect their privacy. While this story is not about an actual individual, it is rooted in the struggles, triumphs, and transformative journeys that many of my clients have experienced.

Each of us has our wake-up calls. Oh boy, let me tell you, waking up to reality is no easy feat. I had to learn this lesson the hard way. I've had my fair share of wake-up calls, and boy, did they shake me to my core! The first one hit me like a ton of bricks when my older brother tragically took his own life. Growing up in a religious household, we were taught to keep our emotions in check, hide our feelings, always put on a brave face, and present a "perfect" image to the world. But let me tell you, bottling up emotions is not the answer. Seeing the devastating effects of anxiety, depression, and addiction firsthand made me realize that these things are real and need to be addressed head-on.

It's easy to numb ourselves and ignore the pain, but that only prolongs the healing process. I've learned that it's essential to take the time to feel our emotions, even the uncomfortable ones so that we can let go and move forward.

My second wake-up call was a real doozy. Cancer. Yeah, you heard that right. Having to break the news to my loved ones was one of the hardest things I've ever had to do. Seeing their tear-filled eyes and feeling their heavy hearts was gut-wrenching. It made me realize how important it is to take control of my health and ensure that I am doing everything in my power to prevent illness and disease and stay healthy for myself and my family.

That experience was a wake-up call that inspired me to take charge of my health and make some changes in my lifestyle. I started eating a whole-food, plant-based diet, exercising regularly, and caring for my mental health. It wasn't easy, but it was necessary and has made all the difference.

So here's the deal. If you're feeling stuck or unsure about how to make a change in your life, know that you're not alone. We all have our wake-up calls—whether it's a tragedy, a health scare, moments of uncertainty, or our world. It's important to remember that every obstacle is an opportunity to grow and learn. We can't just sweep our problems under the rug and hope they go away. Instead, we need to face them and deal with them in a healthy and productive way.

Life has a funny way of waking us up when we need it the most. And while it's not always easy, these wake-up calls can be a blessing in disguise. They remind us of what's truly important and give us the motivation we need to make positive changes in our lives. So don't be afraid to face your wake-up calls head-on, my friend. It's time to wake up and live your best life!

Have you experienced a significant event or circumstance that has caused you to feel a shift in your perspective or priorities?

____

What was the catalyst for this shift?

The catalyst for my "wake-up call happened when ________________

____

____

How did you feel when you received this wake-up call?

I felt ______________________________________

____

____

What changes have you made or want to make because of your wake-up call?

The changes I have made or am willing to make are ______________

____

____

Life's wake-up calls are powerful reminders of your resilience and capacity for growth. They often lead you to reevaluate your priorities, encouraging you to break free from the confines of routine and rediscover your authentic self. Whether it's the laughter of carefree children on a beach or the stark reality of a health scare, these moments compel you to rise, reflect, and redirect your life toward a path of purpose and fulfillment.

Embracing these wake-up calls with courage and an open heart allows you to transform challenges into opportunities for positive change. It's a journey of self-discovery, healing, and self-improvement that ultimately leads to a life filled with authenticity, joy, and endless possibilities. So, my friend, as you encounter your own wake-up calls along life's journey, remember that they are not roadblocks but stepping stones toward a brighter, more meaningful future. It's time for you to wake up and live your best life!

3

Discovering and Embracing Your Core Values

Your values serve as the guiding force that directs the course of your journey.

Living in Alignment

Let's talk about values. What are they? Where do they come from? And why are they important? Knowing and understanding your values is crucial for living a fulfilling and authentic life. Our values function as a compass, guiding us in our decision-making and shaping our behavior. When we live in alignment with our values, we experience a sense of purpose, meaning, and fulfillment. But where do our values come from, and how do we identify them?

Our upbringing, culture, religion, and life experiences often influence our values. We learn what is important to us through our interactions with the world around us. Taking the time to identify and understand our values is a powerful tool for personal growth and transformation.

But the question is, do you know your values? Have you ever taken the time to sit down and really think about what matters most to you in life? What do you stand for? What are the things that you absolutely will not compromise on?

Start by reflecting on your life experiences and what you have learned from them. What experiences have shaped your beliefs and values? What are the principles that you live by? What do you want to stand for in the world? Asking yourself these questions can help you identify and clarify your values.

Now, let's delve into a series of empowering values that serve as our compass, guiding us toward a life aligned with our true selves and fostering deep fulfillment. These values hold immense power and have the potential to transform your life from the inside out. It's not just about understanding these values intellectually but about embodying them fully and allowing them to shape your thoughts, actions, and relationships.

Allow yourself to explore each value in-depth, uncovering its profound impact on your overall well-being and discovering how it can bring authenticity, purpose, and fulfillment into every aspect of your life. Get ready to embrace these values as guiding principles on your personal growth and transformation journey.

Core Values for Authenticity and Fulfillment

1. **Be Your Word.** It's time to channel your inner superhero and embrace integrity and authenticity like never before! Your words are like superpowers—they have the power to build up or tear down. So why not use your powers for good and spread positivity and goodwill wherever you go? And let's not forget about the power of committed action—if you say you're going to do something, you better do it! People will respect your honesty and integrity, and you'll feel like a true hero when you can look in the mirror and say, "I did what I said I was going to do." So go out there, be a superhero of truth and positivity, and watch the world become a better place!
2. **Be Independent.** Listen up, my friend! If you're living your life based on other people's thoughts, then you're living in their dream, not yours. People can be pretty opinionated, but guess what? Their opinions don't define you! It's time to stop trying to please

everyone and start pleasing yourself. Trust your instincts, and don't worry about what others say or do. You're in charge of your own destiny, and you've got all the answers you need. So go out there and be the boss of your life!

3. **Be Clear.** Don't assume anything. Unless, of course, you want to risk looking like a psychic octopus. It's important to ask questions, gather information, and communicate clearly to avoid misunderstanding. Not only will this prevent confusion, but it will also show that you care enough to ensure you're on the same page as everyone else. Plus, who knows what kind of interesting tidbits of knowledge you'll uncover along the way? So speak up and ask away, my friend!
4. **Act With Empathy.** Be an empathetic ninja! Use your emotional intelligence to sense the feelings of others and respect their choices. Remember that everyone has their own unique life story, and they are the experts of their own experiences. By treating others with empathy, you not only create positive relationships but also inspire others to do the same. So go ahead, be the emotional superhero the world needs, and spread some empathy.
5. **Love Yourself.** Listen, you're amazing, just the way you are. So why waste your time judging and sabotaging yourself when you could be out there crushing it? Life is full of obstacles, but you've got this. And remember that it's not about being perfect—it's about doing your best in every moment, no matter what comes your way. So keep that chin up, believe in yourself, and get out there and show the world what you're made of!
6. **Be Accountable.** Alright, let's get real here, my friend. It's time to put on our accountability pants and take responsibility for our lives. Sure, blaming others might be easier, but where's the fun in that? Being accountable means being in control and making things happen. Plus, think about how satisfying it is to own your

accomplishments and take credit for your successes. Let's be adults, put on our big kid pants, and own up to our choices. Trust me; it feels pretty darn good.

Once you have identified your values, it's important to align your actions with them. When our actions are aligned with our values, we experience a sense of purpose and fulfillment. Conversely, when our actions are not aligned with our values, we can experience feelings of guilt, shame, and dissatisfaction.

But what happens when your values conflict with those of others? This is where things can get tricky. It's important to remember that everyone's values are different, and that's okay. We are constantly bombarded with messages from society and the media that can conflict with our values. It's important to stay true to yourself and your beliefs, even in the face of opposition.

One way to stay true to your values is to surround yourself with like-minded people, seeking relationships and communities supporting your values and beliefs. Being part of a community that shares your values can be incredibly empowering and motivating, reinforcing your commitment to living authentically.

Remember that your values are unique to you. Don't compare your values to others or feel pressured to adopt values that don't resonate with you. Instead, embrace your individuality and honor what is important to you.

Take a little time to reflect on your values. Think about the things that make you feel alive, the things that bring you joy and fulfillment, and the things you are passionate about. Write them down and look at them often. Let them guide you in your daily life and decision-making. Remember that values are not set in stone. They can evolve and change over time as we grow and learn. So be open to reevaluating your values and adjusting them as needed.

In the words of the great philosopher Aristotle, "Knowing yourself is the beginning of all wisdom." Take the time to know yourself and your values, and watch as your life transforms in beautiful and meaningful ways.

What are the top five values that guide your life?

My top values are ______________________________

____

____

Where did these values come from?

I learned these values from ______________________________

____

____

How have these values influenced your decisions and actions?

My values have influenced ______________________________

____

____

Have your values ever conflicted with someone else's? How did you manage it?

When my values have conflicted with someone, I have ______________________________

____

____

What communities or relationships can you seek out to support your values?

Other people that I can be in a relationship with that have similar values are

____

____

Are there any values that you want to develop or strengthen in yourself? How can you do that?

The values I would like to strengthen are ____________________________

____

I can strengthen them by ____________________________________

____

____

____

____

Remember that the more you know and honor your values, the more aligned and fulfilled your life will be. So take the time to know yourself and what you stand for, and watch as the world opens to you in beautiful and unexpected ways.

Uncovering Your Inner Drive

Success is an ongoing journey, and failure is not a permanent setback. What truly matters is the courage to persevere and keep moving forward.

Finding Motivation in Your Why

Alright, let's get motivated! Finding your "why" is like finding the secret sauce to success. It's what drives you, gets you out of bed in the morning, and keeps you pushing forward even when the going gets tough.

What's your why? What's the reason behind your dreams and goals? Understanding the purpose behind what you want to achieve is key to staying motivated. It's not just about what you want or how you're going to get it, but it's about the deep-rooted why that keeps you going. Think about it like this: if your goal is to run a marathon, what's your why? Is it to prove to yourself that you can do it? Is it to raise money for a charity close to your heart? Whatever it is, hold onto that why and let it fuel your motivation.

The cool thing about finding your why is that it's unique to you. Nobody else has the same thumbprint, and nobody else has the same why. Take some time to understand yourself and what drives you. It could be a past experience, a future dream, or even a feeling you want to experience.

Once you have a clear and specific why, write it down, put it on a vision board, or make it your phone background. Remind yourself of your why every day and use it as your compass to guide you towards your goals.

Remember that motivation comes from within; finding your why is the key to unlocking that inner drive. Dig deep, get to know yourself, and let your why be your driving force to success!

What makes you feel most alive and fulfilled in life?

I feel most alive when ______________________________________

____

____

What are your biggest passions and interests?

I am enthusiastic and interested in ___________________________

____

____

What are some of the most impactful experiences you've had, and why were they so significant to you?

My most impactful experiences were __________________________

____

____

What are your core values, and how do they guide your decisions and actions?

My core values are ____

____

____

What is happening now in your life?

At home, I am experiencing ______________________________

____

In my relationships, I experience ______________________________

____

____

Others see me as ______________________________

____

____

I see myself as ______________________________

____

____

Physically I feel ______________________________

____

Mentally I feel ______________________________

____

My experience with work is ______________________________

____

____

Financially I ______________________________

____

The effect my current situations have on my life is ____________________

____

____

Find out what you don't want, to know what you do want.

At home, I do not want ____________________

____

At home, I want ____________________

____

____

In my relationships, I do not want ____________________

____

In my relationships, I want to create ____________________

____

____

I don't want others to see me as ____________________

____

I would love it if others saw me as ____________________

____

____

I don't want to see myself as ____

____

I desire to see myself as ____

____

____

Physically I don't want to feel ____

____

I would love my physical body to feel ______________________________________

____

____

Mentally I don't want to feel ____

____

Mentally, I would like to feel ____

____

____

With work, I don't want ____

____

My dream job ____

____

____

Financially I don't want ______________________________________

____

Financially I want to create ___________________________________

____

I know without a doubt that I do not want ______________________

____

____

____

I know I absolutely want ______________________________________

____

____

____

The most important things to me are ____________________________

____

____

The main changes in my life I am considering are _______________

____

____

____

Imagine waking up each morning feeling like you could conquer the world. Think about it —what could you achieve if you could sleep soundly and wake up energized and ready to tackle the day? How would your life change? Picture having a clear mind and all the inner resources you need to manage whatever challenges come your way.

I would experience ______________________________

____

____

Shifting to a healthy lifestyle

What does a healthy life look like to you?

A healthy life consists of, ______________________________

____

____

The health shift that would make a world of difference to me is __________

____

____

Being in vibrant health to me means ______________________________

____

____

Experiencing abundant health would improve my relationships by ________

____

____

The activities I will be able to achieve with a healthier mind and body are

____

____

The projects I will be able to accomplish are _________________________

____

____

Living a healthier lifestyle will allow me to feel ______________________

____

____

Medically speaking, the health benefits I would like to happen would be

____

____

Creating your ideal life

I imagine in my ideal life, I look, feel, and experience __________________

____

____

____

The things that are important to me in my ideal life are _________________

____

____

Right now, in my life, the exact thing I want to create is ______________

____

____

____

____

Why do you want this now? It's not about the *what* or the *how*; it's about your ***why***. Be clear and specific.

The reason ***why****, the purpose of creating this in my life now is to* ________

____

____

____

Let's dig deep into your motivations for creating the life you desire. Don't hold back or try to sugarcoat it—let's get to the root of why you want to make these changes. If weight loss is your goal, ask yourself why you want to lose weight. Is it to feel more confident? To improve your health? To fit into that pair of jeans you've been eyeing?

If you want to reverse a medical condition, ask yourself why that matters. Is it to live a longer, healthier life? To be able to keep up with your kids or grandkids?

If increased energy is what you're after, ask yourself why you want more energy. Is it to be more productive at work? To have more quality time with loved ones? To finally start that hobby you've been putting off?

If creating a better environment is your focus, ask yourself why the climate matters to you. Is it for the sake of future generations? To preserve natural beauty? To reduce pollution and improve air quality?

And if it's the financial success you're seeking, ask yourself what having more money will create for you. Is it the freedom to travel or pursue your passions? The ability to support your family and loved ones? Or perhaps the chance to give back to causes you care about?

Remember that your "why" is the fuel that will keep you motivated and moving forward on your journey toward a healthier, happier life. So don't hold back—dig deep and uncover the true drivers of your desire for change.

Example: I want to release thirty pounds of body weight to create a healthy body where I feel alive and free! I will be able to enjoy an active lifestyle, easily walk along a sandy beach, hike nature's forests, and joyfully play with my kids.

What is your bottom line of *WHY* you want __________ in your life?

I desire ____ *in order to*

create ____

____

Your unique "why" is your guiding star, and it's yours alone. Now that you've defined your "why," inscribe it, visualize it, and make it an integral part of your daily life. Let it be your unwavering compass, leading you toward your goals. Always remember, that motivation springs from within, and in your "why," you hold the key to unlock your greatest potential.

5

Mapping Out Your Goals

"The greater danger for most of us lies not in setting our aim too high and falling short, but in setting our aim too low and achieving our mark."

- Michelangelo

Charting Your Course

Shaping the path to your desired life begins with setting smart and achievable goals. In this chapter, we'll dive into the transformative power of goal setting, specifically focusing on enhancing your mental, physical, and social well-being. It's time to shift your mindset and approach goal setting with a positive outlook that fosters growth and self-compassion.

Rather than fixating on breaking old habits, let's redirect our energy toward embracing new, healthier ones. For instance, instead of reaching for those chips and cookies, let's explore the delicious and nutritious world of fruits and veggies as your go-to snacks. Remember that this journey is not about striving for perfection but embracing progress. Every step forward, no matter how small, deserves to be celebrated. Are you ready to set goals that will propel you toward a vibrant and fulfilling life? Let's dive in.

The best way to achieve big goals is to start small.

"You have the power to move mountains, but you might have to start with a shovel."

Have you ever found yourself dreaming of a big goal but feeling overwhelmed by the enormity of it all? Well, fear not, my friend! The secret is to break it down into bite-sized, achievable steps that keep you motivated and inching closer to your ultimate destination.

Think of it like hiking a mountain—you wouldn't try to tackle the whole thing at once, would you? No way! You start with small, manageable steps, and before you know it, you're at the top, taking in the breathtaking view.

Take my husband and me, for example. We wanted to move from Utah to Hawaii—a big, life-changing goal. But instead of focusing on how hard it would be to leave everything behind, we set our sights on the end goal and worked backward. We identified each small step we needed to take, from researching the islands to finding a house and new jobs.

By setting achievable short-term goals, we didn't feel overwhelmed by the enormity of the task. And guess what? It worked! We were able to move our family, dog, and essentials to Hawaii and create the life we had dreamed of.

But here's the secret: we didn't limit ourselves to a specific plan. Sure, we knew what we wanted, but we stayed open to different possibilities and opportunities. And it paid off, unexpected job offers, a buyer who wanted to buy our furnishings with our home, perfect timing, and a smooth transition to island life.

So don't sell yourself short by only focusing on the big picture. Instead, break it down into achievable steps, stay open to different paths, and watch your dreams become a reality.

Setting the Stage for Success: Preparing to Reach Your Goals

What is the ultimate "big" goal that you want to achieve in your life?

My big goal is ____

____

What small SMART goals can significantly impact you in achieving your larger goal?

Some small goals that can help me in achieving my big goal are __________

____

____

People face many barriers when trying to achieve their goals, such as lack of motivation, fear of failure, limited resources, and unexpected obstacles. Overcoming these barriers requires identifying them and developing strategies to address them. What barriers can you foresee in achieving your goals?

The biggest barriers I may have in achieving my goals are ______________

____

____

What strategies have you found effective in overcoming barriers to achieving your goals?

I can overcome these barriers by ________________________________

____

____

There are multiple strengths that people can use to achieve their goals, some of which include persistence, determination, creativity, discipline, optimism, and adaptability. Additionally, having an unobstructed vision, strong motivation, and a willingness to take risks can also be helpful in overcoming challenges and achieving success. Other essential strengths include self-awareness, the ability to learn from failures and setbacks, and the willingness to seek support and guidance when needed. What are a few of your greatest strengths that will aid you in achieving your goals?

Some of my strengths are ______________________________

____

Taking specific action toward goals means finding the exact steps you need to take to achieve your goals and then taking intentional and focused action to carry out those steps. It's like being a detective and following a trail of clues that will lead you to your ultimate destination. Except instead of solving a crime, you're just trying to accomplish something awesome (but maybe it feels like a crime if it's a really big goal!). And, of course, you won't be wearing a trench coat and fedora, but you can if it makes you feel more focused and motivated!

What are some specific actions you can take to carry out your goals?

Specific actions I can take are ___________________________

____

____

When will you do these specific actions?

I will do these specific actions on ________________________

____

It's important to track progress toward your goal to know if your plan is working. Without monitoring your progress, you won't know if you're on track to achieve your goal or need to adjust your plan to make it more effective.

Don't worry; you don't need a degree in rocket science to monitor your progress. You can simply use a journal, planner, or a high-tech goal-tracking app to keep track of your progress. Who doesn't love a good app? They can remind you of your goals, congratulate you on small victories, and even make you feel guilty for slacking off. With these tools in your arsenal, you can adjust your plan, celebrate small wins, and stay motivated to reach your ultimate life goals.

What are some ways you can monitor your progress?

I will monitor my progress by ____________________________________

____

How can you decide if your plan is effective and if you have successfully achieved your goal?

*I will know when my plan is working when*___________________________

____

____

How often will you review your progress to make sure your plan is working?

I will review my progress as often as _____________________________

____

Having support while pursuing your goals can make all the difference, whether it's a cheerleader, a coach, or a group of like-minded friends.

They can supply encouragement, motivation, and even a swift kick in the pants when needed. Think of them as your personal squad of goal-getters, always ready to lift you up when you're feeling down. Plus, they can offer some much-needed comic relief when the going gets tough. After all, who wouldn't want a friend who can crack a joke about the ridiculousness of burpees or the perils of a juice cleanse? So gather your support team and get ready to conquer those goals with some laughter, sweat, and maybe even a few tears.

Who can you rely on to support you on your path?

The people I can count on to support me in accomplishing my goals are

____

____

How can these people support you?

These people can support me by ________________________________

____

____

It's important to take a moment to reflect and assess your level of commitment and self-belief. This can help you better understand any potential obstacles and make necessary adjustments to your plan. Remember that confidence in yourself is key, and having a positive support system can make a world of difference. So don't be afraid to reach out to friends, family, or even a coach for that extra boost of encouragement and accountability.

How important is this change to you on a scale of 1-10? __________

On that same scale, how confident are you in your ability to achieve this change? ___________ List three ways you can see yourself growing by making this change.

1. ______________________________

2. ______________________________

3. ______________________________

List three ways your lifestyle will improve.

1. ______________________________

2. ______________________________

3. ______________________________

List three ways you can contribute to humanity by doing this.

1. ______________________________

2. ______________________________

3. ______________________________

Setting SMART Goals for Success

Creating SMART goals is the ultimate key to unlocking your potential and living your best life. By being **S**pecific, **M**easurable, **A**ttainable, **R**elevant, and **T**ime-bound, you can create a roadmap to success that will keep you on track and motivated. Writing down your goals and placing them somewhere you can see them daily will also help you stay focused and accountable. So whether your goal is to shed a few pounds, quit smoking, or start a new career, make sure it's SMART, and watch yourself transform into the best version of yourself!

S - Specific. The first step in creating a SMART goal is to make it specific. A specific goal clearly defines what you want to achieve, how you plan to achieve it, and why it's essential. A specific goal is much more achievable than a vague one.

Example: "I want to lose weight" is not specific enough. A more specific goal would be "I want to lose 20 pounds by the end of the year through a combination of exercise and a healthy diet to improve my overall health."

- What specifically do you want to accomplish?

  ____

- How do you plan to achieve it?

  ____

- Why is this goal important to you?

  ____

M - Measurable. The second step in creating a SMART goal is to make it measurable. A measurable goal has clear criteria for success, and you can track your progress along the way. Having measurable goals lets you see how far you've come and how much further you have to go.

Example: "I want to save money" is not measurable. A more measurable goal would be "I want to save $500 per month for the next six months to create an emergency fund."

- How will you measure your progress?

  ____

- What specific criteria will you use to determine success?

  ____

- What milestones will you set along the way?

  ____

A - Achievable. The third step in creating a SMART goal is to make it achievable. An achievable goal is realistic and attainable. Setting unrealistic goals will only lead to frustration and disappointment.

Example: "I want to run a marathon in one month" may not be achievable if you've never run before. A more achievable goal would be "I want to run a 5K in six months by gradually increasing my running distance each week."

- Is this goal realistic, given your current resources and abilities?

  ___

- What steps can you take to make this goal more achievable?

  ___

- What small goals can you set along the way to reach this larger goal?

  ___

R - Relevant. The fourth step in creating a SMART goal is to make it relevant. A relevant goal is meaningful and aligned with your values and priorities.

Example: "I want to learn to play the guitar" may not be relevant if your goal is to become a professional dancer. A more relevant goal would be "I want to improve my flexibility and balance by taking a dance class twice a week for the next six months."

- How does this goal align with your values and priorities?

  ___

- How will this goal contribute to your overall well-being?

  ___

- What impact will achieving this goal have on your life?

____

T - Time-Bound. The final step in creating a SMART goal is to make it time bound. A time-bound goal has a specific deadline or target date. Having a deadline helps you stay focused and motivated, and it also enables you to track your progress.

Example: "I want to learn a new language" may not be time-bound. A more time-bound goal would be "I want to become conversational in Spanish within six months by taking weekly lessons and practicing for at least thirty minutes daily."

- What is the specific target date for achieving this goal?

____

- How long will it take to achieve this goal?

____

- What steps will you take to ensure you meet your goal?

____

Put it all together to create your SMART goal!

Example: "Starting next week, I will commit to practicing meditation for ten minutes daily to reduce stress and increase my sense of calm and inner peace. I will begin with five minutes of meditation each day and gradually increase the time as I become more comfortable with the practice. I will keep a journal of my daily meditation sessions to track my progress. Reducing stress is important to me because it will improve my overall well-being and allow me to be more present and focused on my daily life. I will continue practicing daily meditation for the next thirty days."

Combine every part of your S-M-A-R-T goal and write it down.

*Starting*____

____

____

____

____

____

____

____

____

____

In your journey towards self-improvement and personal growth, setting and pursuing goals is like charting a course for your own adventure. By creating goals, you're not merely wishing for change but actively crafting your future. Whether you're aspiring to improve your career, enhance your health, or enrich your relationships, harness the SMART approach to illuminate your path and bring your ambitions to life. With each goal met you're not only inching closer to your dreams but also learning and growing along the way, making your adventure all the more meaningful. So, set your sights high, map out your goals, and embark on your journey of self-discovery and achievement with unwavering determination

6

Discovering the Depths of Meditation

"How do I know the ways of all things at the beginning?
I look inside myself and see what is within me."

-21st verse The Tao Te Ching

Diving into Stillness

Get ready to embark on a profound journey of self-discovery through the practice of mindfulness and meditation. As you navigate the complexities and uncertainties of our world, mindfulness offers us a powerful tool to find effective and low-cost responses to life's challenges. I invite you to dive into the depths of your being, quiet the constant chatter of your mind, and uncover the transformative power that lies within.

We live in a world where our minds constantly wander, replaying the past or projecting into the future. Our thoughts become an endless stream of worries, plans, and distractions. Each day, it is estimated that we have an average of sixty thousand thoughts, most repetitive and habitual. The problem lies in being trapped in the same cycle of thoughts, preventing us from experiencing true peace and personal growth.

Amidst the noise and chatter of our minds, there is a deeper essence, the authentic self, which exists beyond societal conditioning and life experiences. It is the part of us that remains untouched by external influences, waiting to be awakened. We can tap into this inner sanctuary through mindfulness and meditation and reconnect with our true essence. By letting go of identification with labels and roles, we can embark on a journey of self-discovery.

Mindfulness is not an action we take; it's a state we allow ourselves to enter. It is the art of being fully present in the moment, free from the grip of past regrets or future worries. By quieting the mind, we can access the wisdom and guidance that emanate from our true selves. In this space of inner stillness, we find clarity, peace, and a deep sense of knowledge. We become attuned to the music of our souls, stepping away from the expectations of others and living authentically.

Within each of us lies a noisy chatterbox, a voice constantly telling us what to think, do, and speak. However, we have the power to transcend this chatter and connect with a silent presence that observes without judgment. We can quiet the mind through meditation, creating space to witness our thoughts and emotions without attachment. In this stillness, we come to know our true selves beyond the noise of the inner dialogue.

In the depths of our busy lives, amidst the currents of thoughts and distractions, lies a serene oasis of stillness waiting to be explored. Within the depths of your being, there lies an ocean of infinite potential and tranquility. Just as our bodies are composed primarily of water, so too are our emotions and thoughts like waves that ripple through our inner sea. Meditation allows us to dive deep within ourselves to connect with the calmness and clarity that resides within us. As you embark on this journey of inner exploration, allow yourself to uncover the wisdom and peace found in the depths of your being.

In the vast expanse of your inner ocean, you may sometimes feel like you are swimming alone, navigating the currents of your thoughts and emotions. But fear not, my dear friend, for you can find solace and connect with the depths of your being through meditation. In this tranquil solitude, you can discover the truth of who you are and find the strength to navigate the ebb and flow of life's challenges.

As you immerse yourself in the ocean of love through meditation, know that you are never truly alone. In the depths of your practice, you encounter a boundless connection to the divine, the universe, and all living beings. Within this sacred space, you discover the wellspring of love and compassion, not only for others but also for yourself. Like drops of water merging with the ocean, you will realize that you are never truly alone, love permeates everything, and you are an integral part of this cosmic dance.

Just as two oceans merge into one, we recognize the interconnectedness of our experiences and the oneness that unites us all. Rivers symbolize the flow of life that connects all beings, transcending boundaries, and separations. Through meditation, we tap into the collective wisdom and love that flows through each of us. We recognize that when we can control the inner currents of our thoughts and emotions, we can walk on the water of our own being.

Walking on the water of our own being symbolizes self-mastery and inner alignment. It signifies the integration of our spiritual nature with our human experience. It is a state of harmonious balance where we tap into our highest potential, manifest our authentic selves, and live in alignment with our values and purpose.

When we walk on the water of our own being, we navigate through life with grace and ease. We are no longer tossed around by the turbulent waves of external influences or overwhelmed by our inner turmoil. Instead, we remain anchored in our true essence, connected to the limitless source of love, wisdom, and strength within us. Through the practice of meditation, we can cultivate the ability to walk on the water of our own being and experience the profound transformation that unfolds as we connect with our inner depths.

Imagine descending into a well, deeper, and deeper into the core of your being. As you explore these depths, you unlock a profound reservoir of love, wisdom, and inner peace. It is in this space of stillness and quiet introspection that you gain a heightened awareness of your thoughts, emotions, and the world around you. By journeying inward, you gain the power to navigate the waters of life with grace and resilience. Just like walking on water, when you can control what is happening inside, you can easily navigate any challenge.

I invite you to embrace the transformative power of mindfulness and meditation. Dive into the stillness within, where your inner ocean and the vastness of the universe merge. Discover the profound connection that exists between all beings and allow love and compassion to flow through every aspect of your life. Remember that you are a unique embodiment of the divine, and by diving deep into the waters of meditation, you unlock the boundless potential and peace that exists within you.

Take time each day to sit in silence, go deep within the layers of your mind, and enter the peaceful space between the noise and thoughts. In this space, you will discover the essence of your being, your true self, and the symphony of your soul. It may require effort and practice, but remember that the connection with your inner self is always there, waiting for you to tune in and listen.

Different Pathways to Mindfulness

Explore the depths of mindfulness through various practices that invite you to engage your senses, connect with your heart, and find inner stillness. These pathways offer unique perspectives and opportunities for self-discovery, allowing you to navigate the ocean of your being with grace and tranquility.

- **Sensory Awareness**: Dive into the richness of the present moment by focusing on your senses. Take time to truly see, hear, smell, taste, and touch the world around you. Notice the details, colors, sounds, and textures. Engage in activities that awaken your senses, such as savoring a delicious meal, listening to soothing music, or enjoying the fragrance of flowers. As you explore sensory awareness, consider incorporating walking meditation into your practice. Take slow, deliberate steps, feeling the sensation of your feet connecting to the earth as if kissing the ground with each step. Allow the experience of walking to become a mindful journey, where you fully immerse yourself in the present moment, attuned to the sensations, sounds, and sights surrounding you. This practice not only cultivates mindfulness but also helps reduce stress, increase focus, and heighten your overall sense of presence.

- **Mind-Body Connection:** Create a bridge between your mind and body through a simple yet powerful exercise. Trace the outline of your hand on a piece of paper and fill it with symbols, words, or images that represent your favorite activities, people, places, and things. As you trace your hand, synchronize your breath with a pattern of inhaling for four counts, holding for seven counts, and exhaling for eight counts. This practice promotes relaxation, reduces stress, and fosters deep inner peace.
- **Guided Visualization:** Embark on a journey of the imagination through guided visualizations. These powerful narratives guide you into a state of deep relaxation and heightened awareness, allowing you to tap into your subconscious mind and access your innate wisdom. Choose visualizations that resonate with your intentions and desires, whether it be self-love, abundance, clarity, or personal transformation. Let your mind's eye be your compass as you explore the vast realms of possibility within.
- **Loving Kindness:** Open your heart to the practice of loving-kindness meditation, a beautiful way to cultivate compassion and empathy. Begin by closing your eyes and recalling someone who could receive assistance from kindness, love, and understanding. Extend your heartfelt intention towards them, wishing them well-being, happiness, and peace. As you continue this practice, expand

your loving energy to encompass all living beings, sending waves of love and compassion throughout the world. This practice not only benefits others but also nourishes your own soul.

- **Mindfulness in Daily Activities**: Discover mindfulness in the mundane by incorporating it into your daily routines. Whether taking a shower, walking, or even eating, bring your full attention to the experience. Notice the sensation of water on your skin, the rhythm of your steps, or the flavors and textures of the food you consume. By infusing mindfulness into these activities, you elevate them from mere chores to moments of deep presence and connection.
- **Clearing Meditation**: Just as we open a window to circulate fresh air in a stuffy room, we can do the same for our minds. Start by focusing on your breath, inhaling deeply, and exhaling slowly. Imagine fresh, cool air entering your head and swirling around your brain, collecting any worries or heaviness. Visualize these burdensome thoughts and emotions leaving your body through your nose and ears with each exhale. As you continue this practice, feel the lightness and clarity that comes with releasing what no longer serves you.

Explore these pathways to mindfulness and find the ones that resonate with you. Remember that there are many more practices to explore, such as Zen meditation, mantra meditation, yoga, chakra meditation, qigong meditation, and sound bath meditation. Each offers its own unique way of deepening your connection with yourself and the present moment. So dive in and let the currents of mindfulness guide you to a place of inner peace, clarity, and profound self-discovery.

Reflect on a recent experience when you felt overwhelmed or stressed. How might practicing mindfulness and meditation have helped you navigate that situation more calmly and resiliently?

*These practices can be powerful tools for managing stress by*_____________

____

Consider the benefits of regular meditation practice on your mental and emotional well-being. How might cultivating mindfulness and inner stillness contribute to greater clarity, focus, and emotional resilience in your daily life?

The positive transformations that can unfold through consistent practice are

____

Reflect on the moments in your day when you feel most present and engaged with the present moment. What activities or experiences help you cultivate mindfulness naturally?

*I feel most present in the moment when*____________________________

____

____

How can you incorporate these moments of mindfulness into your formal meditation practice?

I can incorporate these moments into my meditation practice by __________

____

____

Consider the concept of self-care and nurturing your well-being. How might carving out time for meditation and mindfulness be an act of self-love and self-compassion?

These practices can support my overall health and happiness in many ways, such as

____

____

Reflect on the power of the present moment. How often do you dwell on the past or worry about the future? Consider the freedom and liberation from anchoring yourself in the present moment through meditation and mindfulness.

I dwell on the past or worry about the future ______________________.

By shifting my awareness, my well-being will be ____________________

____

As you venture forward, may mindfulness and meditation be your faithful companions, guiding you toward a life filled with greater presence, purpose, and boundless possibilities. Dive into the stillness within, for there, you'll find the adventure of a lifetime—the adventure of discovering the true you.

7

Embracing Commitment for Lasting Change

"If it's to be, it's up to me and my committed action."

Taking the Leap

Alright, listen up my friend! If you want to make a significant lifestyle change and start living your best, healthiest life, it's time to understand the importance and meaning of taking committed action. Reading self-help books and gaining knowledge is undoubtedly valuable, but it's the action that truly brings about transformative results.

Wholeheartedly committing to the life you aspire to create involves making a firm decision to prioritize your well-being. It's about recognizing that your health and happiness are worth the effort and dedication. Even the best intentions can fade without commitment, leaving you stuck in the same old patterns.

Taking action is where the rubber meets the road. It's the moment when you turn your aspirations into reality. It requires stepping out of your comfort zone, embracing challenges, and pushing through resistance. Taking committed action means putting in the work consistently, even when motivation wanes or obstacles arise.

When you take committed action, you send a powerful message to yourself and the universe that you are serious about your goals. It's a declaration that you are ready to invest your time, energy, and resources into creating positive change in your life. Each step forward becomes a building block in the foundation of your success.

Taking committed action also builds momentum. Each step you take fuels the next, creating a ripple effect of progress. It's like pushing a boulder up a hill—it may be challenging at first, but you gain strength and momentum with each push. Before you know it, you'll find yourself at the top, looking back at how far you've come.

Committing to taking action also fosters accountability. When you make a commitment, you hold yourself responsible for following through. It's about being true to your word and honoring the promises you make to yourself. Accountability breeds integrity and builds self-confidence as you prove to yourself that you are capable of following through on your intentions.

Ultimately, taking committed action is a powerful catalyst for personal growth and transformation. It propels you forward, allowing you to surpass limitations and discover the depths of your potential. With each action you take, you become the driver of your destiny, shaping your desired life. So let's get to it! Make that commitment and start taking action towards your goals. Your future self will thank you for it!

On a scale of 1-10, what is your level of commitment to achieving your goals? _________

If you are at ten, that's fantastic! Congratulations, you are fully committed to achieving your goals. However, if you are at a lower number, ask yourself why you gave yourself that rating. Be honest with yourself, as acknowledging your current level of commitment is the first step in making progress.

I gave myself the number _________ *because* _________________________

____

____

Once you've identified why you are not fully committed, think about what would have to happen for you to give yourself a ten. What needs to change? What motivates you? What do you need to do to get there?

I would give myself a ten if I fully committed to ____________________.

Finally, make an action plan. What steps can you take to fully commit to achieving your goals? Write down specific actions and hold yourself accountable for following through.

The actions I will take to commit myself fully are ____________________

____

____

Commitment and action are the keys to achieving your goals and living your best life. It's not enough to simply desire change or wish for a better future. You must make a conscious decision to commit to your goals and take consistent action toward them. Without commitment, your goals remain distant dreams; without action, they remain stagnant ideas. The combination of commitment and action propels you forward, allowing you to overcome challenges, grow, and transform.

All-In: Making a Pledge of Commitment to Your Goals

I am committed to: ____

____

____

Realistically, by committing to this, what will your life look like in a year?

*By taking committed action, the changes I will experience in my life one year from now will be*____

____

____

Five years from now ____

____

____

Ten years from now ____

____

____

Embrace the journey ahead, knowing that each step you take brings you closer to the life you envision. Remember that it's not about perfection but about progress. Celebrate each action, no matter how small, and let them propel you towards a healthier, happier, and more fulfilled version of yourself. The power is in your hands, so go forth and ignite your inner drive through committed action!

8

No More Excuses

"If you could kick the person in the pants responsible for most of your trouble, you wouldn't sit for a month."

-Theodore Roosevelt

Mastering Accountability

Once upon a time, there was a woman who I will refer to as Lily, who was molested as a child. For years, she was the victim and allowed her past trauma to define her life. She struggled with depression and anxiety and often found herself in toxic relationships. But one day, Lily realized she was the only one who could take control of her life and break the cycle of victimhood.

She began to take accountability for her own happiness and well-being. She sought therapy and support groups to work through her trauma and learn healthy coping mechanisms. She also consciously surrounded herself with positive and supportive people who uplifted and encouraged her.

Through this process, Lily discovered a strength within her that she never knew existed. She learned that she could take control of her life and make it what she wanted. She also realized that her past trauma did not define her and that she had the power to create her own identity.

As Lily continued her journey of self-discovery and accountability, she learned a valuable lesson. She realized that while she couldn't change what had happened to her in the past, she could control how she reacted to it and how she allowed it to shape her future. Through her own resilience and determination, she was able to break free from the cycle of victimhood and live a fulfilling and joyful life.

Disclaimer Note: The client story presented above is a fictionalized composite of experiences from multiple clients I have worked with. Names, identifying details, and specific circumstances have been changed to protect their privacy. While this story is not about an actual individual, it is rooted in the struggles, triumphs, and transformative journeys that many of my clients have experienced.

Lily's story serves as a reminder that no matter what life throws at us, we have the power to take accountability and create the life we want. We may not be able to control everything that happens to us, but we can always control how we respond. And when we take responsibility for our own happiness and well-being, we can overcome any obstacle and achieve our dreams.

You, my friend, hold the power to shape your own destiny. You have the ability to influence, direct, and take charge of your environment. Your life is a canvas, and you are the artist who can paint it in any color and shape that you wish. Accountability is not just a word. It's a state of being. It's the ability to recognize that you are the creator of your own reality and that you have the power to manifest your dreams into reality. It's about being aware of your thoughts, feelings, and actions and taking ownership of them, no matter the outcome. Accountability is the ultimate expression of self-love and self-respect, for it empowers you to take charge of your life and steer it in the direction that you desire.

You see, accountability is about taking ownership of your life and your choices. It's about recognizing that you have the power to create your reality and that every thought, word, and action you take impacts the world around you. Psychologists call this the "locus of control," or the degree to which you believe you have control over the events in your life. When you have an internal locus of control, you recognize that you are in the driver's seat and have the power to steer your life in any direction you choose.

But accountability isn't just about psychology. It's also about physics. You see, everything in the universe is connected, and every action you take creates a ripple effect that spreads out into the world. As Newton's third law of motion states, "For every action, there is an equal and opposite reaction." When you take responsibility for your life and choices, you are not only influencing your own reality but also contributing to the world's collective consciousness.

Now, I know that taking accountability for your life can be a daunting task. It requires courage, self-awareness, and a willingness to face your fears and limitations. But it's also one of the most empowering things you can do for yourself. When you take ownership of your life, you free yourself from the chains of victimhood and powerlessness. You become the captain of your ship, navigating the seas of life with confidence and purpose. And that, my friend, is a beautiful thing.

You have the power to choose how you respond to any situation. You can cast yourself as the victim, pointing fingers at others, or you can seize control of your destiny, accepting full responsibility. It's not always easy, but it's always worth it.

Take a moment to reflect on a situation where you may have been the victim and blamed someone else for your circumstances. Write down who or what you accused and why.

I blamed ____ *for*

____

because ____.

Now, ask yourself, how did you contribute to the situation? Write down your role in the situation.

I contributed to the situation by ___________________________

____.

Next, identify the lesson you can learn from this situation. How can you use this experience to grow and improve?

The lesson I can learn from this situation is ___________________

____.

Finally, commit to taking action and being accountable for your life moving forward. Write down one small step you can take today to move towards your goals.

One small action I can take today is _______________________

____.

Taking accountability for your life is a process. It's not something that happens overnight, but it's something you can work on every day. And as you do, you'll start to see positive changes and growth in all areas of your life.

9

Inner GPS

"There is a law in psychology that if you form a picture in your mind of what you would like to be, and you keep and hold that picture there long enough, you will soon become exactly as you have been thinking."

-William James

Navigating the Highway of Self-Discovery

Let's kickstart this journey by establishing a strong, unwavering intention for personal growth, healing, and transformation. Visualize this intention as programming your internal navigation system, charting the course toward your ideal life filled with wellness and joy. Without a clear destination, you're liable to end up on any old path, and frankly, we're not interested in aimless wandering. Your intention is the North Star in your night sky, the beacon amidst stormy seas. It's the burning "why" that fuels your determination, pushing you forward when the terrain gets rocky. And let's be honest—it'll resemble Mount Everest at times. Yet always remember that within you resides a resilience stronger than any obstacle you'll encounter.

THE POWER OF INTENTION AND THE LAW OF ATTRACTION

You get what you think about most of the time.
Words create Thoughts and Feelings.
Thoughts and Feelings Create Vibrations.
Vibrations Create Actions.
Actions Create Results

The power of intention is a fascinating concept. It's like a magic wand that we all have but may not realize how to use effectively. When you set an intention, you are essentially sending out a signal to the universe that says, "This is what I want to create." And the universe responds by aligning the people, situations, and resources necessary to make that intention a reality.

Now, let's talk about the law of attraction. It may sound a bit woo-woo, but there's actually a scientific basis for it. This law states that like attracts like—in other words, your thoughts and emotions create your reality. When you focus on negative thoughts and feelings, you attract more negativity into your life. But when you focus on positive thoughts and feelings, you attract positivity.

The physics behind this is simple: everything in the universe is made up of energy, and energy vibrates at different frequencies. When you focus on positive thoughts and feelings, you raise your vibrational frequency, attracting other high-frequency energy to you. It's like tuning into a particular radio station—you can only hear the music if you're tuned to the right frequency.

From a psychological perspective, the power of intention and the law of attraction can help you shift your mindset from victim to creator. Instead of feeling like life is happening to you, you can take control and actively create the life you want. And when you start seeing positive results from your intentions, it becomes a self-fulfilling cycle of positivity.

So set your intentions high and focus on positive thoughts and feelings. You may be surprised at what the universe has in store for you!

Manifest your life according to your intentions.

Clear Intention + Committed Action = Results

"I deserve and accept all good in my life."

Are you ready to manifest your dreams into reality? Get ready to use the power of visualization and intention to create the life you want. But before you start writing down your goals and desires, take a moment to relax and breathe. Inhale the good vibes and exhale the bad.

Now, close your eyes and visualize your ideal life. See yourself in the best possible version of yourself. Feel the excitement, the joy, the love, and the abundance surrounding you.

Then, take deep breaths and imagine yourself achieving your goals effortlessly.

As you open your eyes, grab a pen, and start writing down what you want. Be specific and detailed in your descriptions. Include all areas of your life, including your health, relationships, career, and finances.

Remember to focus on what you want, not what you don't want. Don't waste your energy and time on negative thoughts and emotions. Instead, channel your energy and focus on the positive aspects of your life.

As you draft your new story, keep breathing and stay relaxed. Let go of any doubts, fears, and limiting beliefs that may hold you back. Surrender to the Universe and trust that everything will work out for your highest good.

And most importantly, be open to new possibilities and opportunities that may come your way. The Universe has a way of bringing what you want into your life, sometimes in unexpected ways. So stay positive, stay focused, and stay open to receiving all the abundance and blessings that come your way.

I, ______________________________ now have a beautiful healthy life …

After writing your story, please close your eyes, take three big deep breaths, and visualize every aspect of it again.

Charting the Course: Visualizing Your Grand Adventure

Your thoughts are the architects of your life. Where your attention goes, energy follows, shaping your reality.

Vision boards help to clarify and manifest one's goals and desires. Focusing on the things you want in your life creates a positive energy that can attract those things to you. By creating a visual representation of your goals and desires, you are reminding yourself of what you truly want, and it becomes easier to stay focused and motivated to achieve them. Additionally, a vision board can help you to stay inspired and creative in finding ways to make your dreams a reality. It is a constant reminder of what you are working towards and can help you make decisions that align with your goals.

So let's get crafty and create a vision board for your ideal healthy life! Don't worry; you don't need to be a Picasso to make this happen. All you need is some magazines, glue, and a poster board.

Think about what you really want in life. Do you want to run a marathon? Do you want to eat healthier? Do you want to have more peace and balance in your life? Whatever it is, find pictures and words in those magazines that represent your dreams and aspirations. And don't forget to use some sparkly glitter glue for that extra pizzazz.

Once you've finished your masterpiece, display it somewhere you'll see it daily. And whenever you look at it, take a moment to really imagine yourself living that life. You'll be surprised how powerful this visual representation can be in helping you attract the healthy life you desire.

Let's get those scissors and glue ready and start creating your own vision board. Who knows, maybe you'll discover your hidden artistic talent along the way!

10

Crafting Conscious Thoughts and Communication

"Whether you think you can, or you think you can't – you're right,"

-Henry Ford

Words Create Worlds

Eliminating doubt and shifting it into knowing is essential for successful manifestation. Great manifestors are grounded in unwavering faith and a strong belief in their desires. They understand that doubt only serves as a roadblock on the path to manifestation. When Jesus healed the man, he didn't doubt for a moment that he would be healed; he knew it with absolute certainty. Jesus didn't approach him with uncertainty and say, "Well, I'll give it a shot, but I'm not sure if it will work." Instead, he confidently approached him, knowing he could heal him. Like Jesus, you can approach your desires with unwavering confidence and belief.

One powerful technique to eliminate doubt and reinforce your beliefs is using "I am" statements. These statements serve as affirmations that reflect your authentic essence and the reality you wish to manifest. By declaring "I am," you align yourself with the qualities, experiences, and outcomes you desire to attract into your life.

"I am" statements are empowering because they operate on the principle of self-identification. When you use "I am" followed by a positive attribute or desired state, you declare and claim that reality is your own.

For example, saying "I am confident," "I am abundant," or "I am healthy" affirms and reinforces those qualities within yourself.

When crafting your "I am" statements, it's essential to focus on the positive and state them in the present tense. This helps shift your subconscious mind and align your thoughts and emotions with the desired reality. By consistently repeating these statements and embodying the qualities they stand for, you are programming your mind to manifest those experiences into your life.

Remember that the power of "I am" lies in your belief and conviction behind the statements. It's not just about repeating words; it's about feeling and embodying the truth of those statements. When you genuinely believe in the power of "I am" and align your actions and thoughts with your affirmations, you activate the law of attraction and open yourself up to the limitless possibilities of manifestation.

As you integrate "I am" statements into your manifestation practice, be intentional and specific with your affirmations. Choose words that resonate deeply with you and reflect the reality you desire to create. Repeat them daily, visualize yourself embodying those qualities, and allow yourself to feel the emotions associated with living that reality.

Embracing "I am" statements as part of your manifestation practice empowers you to step into your true power and create your desired life. Trust in the process, believe in your affirmations and watch as your reality begins to align with your deepest desires. You have the ability to manifest and create a life filled with abundance, joy, and fulfillment. To manifest your desires, you must practice phrasing your requests in a way that ends doubt. Use words such as "I will" and "I am" to affirm your beliefs and expectations. This language reflects your confidence and faith in your ability to manifest your desires.

Take a moment to think about your desires and goals. Phrase them in a way that eliminates doubt and affirms your belief in their attainment. Use words such as "I will" and "I am" to speak your desires into existence.

Remember that doubt is the enemy of manifestation, and faith is the key to success.

Write down a statement that affirms your belief and eliminates doubt.

Example: "I will confidently and joyfully manifest my desires, knowing that the Universe is working in my favor."

I will ____

____

____

Get ready to stir up some godlike nature within yourself by playing around with the power of "I AM" statements. But first, a warning, be careful what you attach those two little words to because they hold some serious weight.

If you go around saying, "I am a hot mess," or "I am a disaster," or "I am a walking potato," then you're just inviting trouble, my friend. The Universe has no choice but to give you what you ask for, so don't waste your divine power on negative nonsense.

Instead, let's turn up the positivity dial and make some powerful "I AM" statements. Even if it initially feels silly, trust the process. Say it: "I AM awesome." "I AM successful." "I AM healthy." "I AM a freakin' rockstar."

Now, don't just say it and forget it. Write those statements down, put them on a sticky note on your bathroom mirror, or set them as reminders on your phone. Please keep them in your awareness and watch as the Universe starts to deliver the goods.

I am ____

I am ____

I am ____

____

Words have a powerful impact on our lives, and the words we choose to speak can either lift us up or bring us down. When we use words of increase, we talk of our blessings, successes, and the good news in every situation. We use positive comments with love to uplift people and tell them how beautiful and amazing they are to have in our lives. This creates a positive and uplifting environment for us and those around us.

On the other hand, words of decrease focus on our problems, fears, pains, sicknesses, failures, judgments of people, gossip, and bad news. These words can create a hostile and draining environment. For example, if someone constantly tells you you're not good enough, ugly, or stupid, those are all terrible words of decrease that can make you feel bad about yourself and lower your self-esteem.

Let's turn up the volume on words of increase and turn down the volume on words of decrease, shall we? It's time to start spreading positive vibes and uplifting energy everywhere we go.

It's important to be mindful of our words and how they impact us and those around us. By practicing using words of increase, we can create a more positive and uplifting environment for ourselves and others. Take some time to think about the words you use and how you can shift them to be more positive and uplifting.

Write down a list of negative words or phrases you use often, then write a positive alternative to replace them. For example, instead of saying, "I'm so stressed out," say, "I'm feeling challenged, but I know I can manage it." Instead of saying, "I hate Mondays," say, "I'm excited to start a new week and see what opportunities come my way."

Instead of thinking "___________"	*Say "___________________"*
___________________________	___________________________
___________________________	___________________________
___________________________	___________________________
___________________________	___________________________
___________________________	___________________________
___________________________	___________________________
___________________________	___________________________

11

Whole-istic Nourishment

"It is health that is real wealth and not pieces of gold and silver."

-Mahatma Gandhi

Fueling Mind, Body, and Spirit

Once upon a time, there was a man who took excellent care of his car. He would always fill it up with premium fuel, take it for regular maintenance, and keep it sparkling clean. One day, his friend commented, "Wow, you take such great care of your car. It looks and runs better than ever. I wish I could take care of my body the same way you take care of your car."

The man was struck by this comment and thought, "Why do we take better care of our cars than our own bodies?" He realized that just like a car needs the right kind of fuel to run properly, our bodies also need proper nourishment to function at their best.

From that day on, the man made a commitment to take care of his body the same way he took care of his car. He started fueling his body with nutrient-dense foods, getting regular exercise, and taking time to rest and recharge. As a result, he felt better than ever, with more energy, mental clarity, and overall health.

He shared his experience with his friend and encouraged him to do the same. "Think of your body as your most valuable asset, just like your car," he said. "You wouldn't put dirty fuel in your car and expect it to run well, so why put junk in your body and expect it to function properly?"

The friend was inspired by the man's words and decided to make a change. He started eating healthier foods, drinking more water, and exercising regularly. Over time, he noticed a significant improvement in his overall health and well-being.

The man and his friend both realized that just like a car, our bodies need proper care and maintenance to function at their best. By fueling our bodies with nutrient-dense foods and caring for our physical and mental health, we can improve our quality of life and feel our best every day.

So the next time you're deciding what to eat or whether to exercise, remember this story. Your body is your vehicle for life, and just like a car, it needs proper fuel and maintenance to run smoothly. Take care of your body, and it will take care of you.

It's time to ask yourself, what do you really need from food? Is it just something to keep you from feeling hungry, or is it fuel to keep your body running like a well-oiled machine? Just like a car needs the right fuel to run efficiently and avoid breaking down, your body needs the right fuel to function at its best.

Start by looking at your current diet. Are you fueling your body with nutrient-dense foods like fresh fruits and vegetables, lean proteins, and healthy fats? Or are you filling up on processed foods that are high in sugar, salt, and unhealthy fats?

Do you sometimes feel lost in the maze of food choices and like you need a degree in nutrition just to figure out what to eat for dinner? Fear not! You're not alone.

It's easy to get caught up in the hype and marketing of the food industry and fall into the trap of convenience fast food, but the long-term effects can be detrimental to your health. So take a step back and think about the long-term benefits of fueling your body with healthy, whole foods. Not only will it help prevent chronic diseases and support a healthy weight, but it can also improve your mental clarity and overall mood.

It's time to take charge of your health and happiness. Do your research and educate yourself on the power of whole, natural foods. Then, choose nutrient-dense options like colorful fruits and veggies, healthy fats, and lean proteins.

Commit yourself to choosing nourishing and healthy foods for your mind and body. Start by incorporating more whole foods into your diet and try cooking meals at home with fresh ingredients. Remember that the food choices you make today will affect your health tomorrow. It's time to start treating our bodies and minds like the beautiful, powerful machines they are.

Choose fuel that your body will thank you for and help you shine, both inside and out.

What benefits do you hope to gain from fueling your body with healthy whole foods?

*The benefits I look forward to are*______________________________

____

What foods genuinely nourish your mind and body and give you a sense of inner satisfaction?

The foods that nourish my mind and body the best is ________________

____

____

What foods do you feel good eating?

I feel good when I eat ______________________________________

____

What does it feel like to be nourished with healthy food?

When I eat healthy food, I feel _______________________________

____

What do healthy, nourishing foods look, smell, feel, and taste like?

Healthy, nourishing foods look like ______________________________

____

Smell like ____

Feel like ____

*Taste like*____

Where do healthy foods come from?

Healthy food comes from ______________________________________

It turns out that some of the foods we thought were healthy may actually be contributing to environmental damage. For example, did you know that almond milk takes an enormous amount of water to produce, and that some farms in California have drained their aquifers to grow almonds for export to other countries? Similarly, the production of palm oil, a commonly used ingredient in many processed foods, has led to widespread deforestation in Southeast Asia, causing significant harm to wildlife habitats and contributing to climate change.

And don't even get me started on the environmental impact of meat and dairy production. The meat industry is one of the most significant contributors to greenhouse gas emissions, and the waste produced by factory farming pollutes our air and water. Consuming animal products can also negatively affect animal welfare and human health. Animals raised for meat and dairy are often kept in crowded and inhumane conditions, leading to stress, disease, and decreased quality of life. The heavy use of antibiotics and hormones in animal agriculture also contributes to the development of antibiotic-resistant bacteria and can have negative health effects on those consuming the products.

But don't worry, it's not all doom and gloom! Choosing organic, local, and in-season plant-based foods can improve your health, reduce your carbon footprint, and support sustainable farming practices. Additionally, limiting meat consumption and choosing plant-based options can significantly reduce your impact on the environment and promote the ethical treatment of animals.

Dear friend, please make conscious choices about what you eat and take the time to understand how your food choices impact the environment, animals, and your health. Educate yourself on sustainable and ethical farming practices and choose foods that align with your values. Not only will you be supporting your own health, but you will be doing your part to protect our planet for future generations.

What plant-based options are locally sourced and minimally processed in your area?

Some plant-based options available to me are ______________________

____

How can you incorporate more sustainable and ethical food choices into your daily life?

I can choose foods ______________________________________

____

Have you ever considered reducing or eliminating your consumption of animal products?

What are some reasons you might consider doing so?

I would consider reducing or eliminating eating meat and dairy products because ______________________________________

____

____

What are some nutritious breakfasts, lunch, dinner, and snack foods that are healthy for you and the earth that you can incorporate into your diet?

Some healthy foods I can eat for breakfast are ______________________

____

____

A few nutritious lunches I can eat are ______________________

____

____

Some healthy dinner ideas I have are ______________________

____

____

A few nutritious snacks I can have on hand are ______________________

____

____

How can you make healthier choices when eating out or on the go?

When eating out or on the go, I will ______________________

____

What are some challenges you may face in changing your diet?

The challenges I might have include ______________________

____

How can you overcome those challenges?

I can prepare myself and overcome the challenges by ____________________

____

Food is not the only thing you consume that can affect your energy, how you feel, and how you live. Let's face it—we all have our guilty pleasures when it comes to what we listen to and watch. But have you ever stopped to think about how it affects your mood and energy levels? Watching a horror movie or listening to death metal might give you a temporary thrill, but what effect does it have on your mind and body in the long run?

On the other hand, when we listen to positive music and inspiring talks and surround ourselves with happy people, it's like a breath of fresh air for our minds and bodies. Our energy levels rise, and suddenly everything seems possible.

It's not just about what we listen to and watch, either. The people we spend time with, the conversations we have, and even the thoughts we think can all profoundly affect our overall well-being.

What changes can you make today to ensure that everything you consume nourishes your mind, body, and spirit? Maybe it's time to start listening to more positive podcasts or surrounding yourself with people who inspire you. Perhaps it's time to take a break from social media or limit your exposure to negative news. Remember, you have the power to choose what you consume. Make conscious choices that uplift and energize you, and watch as your life begins to transform.

Inventory everything you've consumed today, from food to media to conversations. What was nourishing, and what wasn't?

Nourishing: ____

____

Not nourishing: ____

____

What changes can you make tomorrow to ensure that everything you consume supports your well-being?

The changes I can make ______________________________________

____

____

How does the music you listen to affect your mood and energy levels?

*My music affects me by*______________________________________

____

What positive podcasts or audiobooks could you incorporate into your daily routine?

Some positive books and podcasts ______________________________

____

How can you surround yourself with more positive people and reduce your exposure to Negativity?

I can surround myself with ____________________________________

In the grand adventure of life, the story you've been crafting has now reached a turning point. As you ponder your choices in food, entertainment, and the world around you, remember that every decision holds the power to shape not only your health and well-being but also the world we all share. It's a reminder that the adventure of self-discovery extends beyond the boundaries of your own experiences; it's intertwined with the intricate tapestry of our planet and all living beings. So, as you savor each bite, listen to each note, and engage in each conversation, do so with intention and awareness. Embrace the journey of mindful consumption, and in doing so, you not only nourish your body, mind, and spirit but also contribute to a brighter, more harmonious world for us all.

12

Journey Towards Freedom from Addictions

"I truly understood myself only after going through a period of self-destruction. It was during the process of fixing myself that I discovered my real identity."

- Anonymous

Escaping the Monkey Trap

Once upon a time, there was a mischievous little monkey who loved nothing more than his beloved peanuts. This monkey was smart, quick, and always on the lookout for a delicious snack. One day, he stumbled upon a gourd filled to the brim with delicious nuts. His heart raced with excitement, and his mouth salivated at the thought of getting his hands on the peanuts. Without hesitation, the monkey plunged his tiny hand into the gourd and grabbed a fistful of peanuts. But as he tried to withdraw his hand, he found himself trapped, unable to remove his clenched fist from the gourd. The more he pulled and tugged, the more he injured his arm and wrist.

The monkey was so obsessed with his precious peanuts that he didn't even think to let go and set himself free. He could have saved himself a lot of pain and suffering if he had just released his grip and let go of the peanuts.

The monkey story is a perfect illustration of how we humans are sometimes trapped by our addictions. It could be an addiction to food, drugs, alcohol, or even social media. We become so attached to these things that we forget we have the power to let go and free ourselves.

It's easy to overlook the addictions we face in our daily lives. We often cling to things that are not good for us, whether it's an unhealthy relationship, a toxic job, or unpleasant habits that hold us back. Perhaps we don't consider scrolling through Instagram for hours or binging on junk food as an addiction. But the truth is, these habits can be just as harmful as more obvious addictions.

Food addiction is a genuine challenge for numerous individuals and can be among the most difficult addictions to combat. Just as it's unwise to offer alcohol to someone recovering from alcoholism, it's equally inconsiderate to tempt someone with a food addiction by offering them sugary treats or junk food. And just like any addiction, it's important to recognize the root cause and work towards true healing and happiness.

But addiction goes beyond just substances. Saying "yes" to everything can also be a form of addiction. It's not just the word "yes," but the approval and avoidance of confrontation that becomes addicting. Being honest with yourself and others about what you genuinely want is essential.

We all have our own version of peanuts that we cling to, and that is perfectly normal. It's important to recognize that addiction is a part of the human experience. The key is to be aware of these addictions and work towards freeing ourselves from their grip.

One of the most common addictions is procrastination. We put things off until the last minute, then feel guilty and overwhelmed. Another common addiction is our addiction to technology. We're glued to our phones and social media, often at the expense of real-life interactions and experiences.

Addictions can be overcome. It starts with the willingness to let go of the peanuts that are holding us back. We can replace unhealthy habits with healthier ones, focus on our passions and goals, and surround ourselves with positive influences.

As Deepak Chopra said, addiction is an unrecognized spiritual craving. It's not just about physical pleasure but about finding true joy and purpose in life. By overcoming our addictions, we can unlock our full potential and live a life of freedom and abundance.

My friend, I challenge you to take a look at your own life and see where you might be holding onto peanuts. What habits keep you trapped and prevent you from living your best life? It's time to let go and set yourself free. Anything is possible with a bit of motivation, inspiration, and willingness to let go.

1. **Acknowledge your addiction.** Releasing an addiction is not an easy feat, but it all starts with acknowledging its existence. This requires a great deal of inner strength and courage. To take the first step towards recovery, you need to look at the places in your life where you feel powerless and find the parts of you that are out of control. What are your "peanuts" in life that you are holding onto? What are the things that have gotten out of hand and are hindering your growth and progress? It's time to face these questions with honesty and begin the journey toward breaking free from your addiction.

I am addicted to ____

____

Acknowledging the adverse effects of your addiction may be difficult, but it's a necessary step in breaking free from it. Writing down a list of all the adverse effects your addiction has caused can serve as a powerful motivator to quit.

Take some time to reflect on why you picked up your "peanuts" in the first place. Was it to cope with stress, anxiety, or depression? Did you start using it to fit in with a particular group of people? Were you seeking a temporary escape from reality? By understanding the root cause of your addiction, you can begin to address it and find healthier coping mechanisms. Why did you pick up your "peanuts" in the first place?

I first started ________________________ *because* ____________________

____

____

I first became addicted when ____

____

____

My addiction is preventing me from __________________________________

____

____

I became addicted because it makes me feel ___________________________

____

I am satisfied from my addiction when _______________________________

____

Have you ever stopped to think about how your addictions may affect your health? Are you at a greater risk of getting a sexually transmitted disease, cancer, heart disease, or another illness due to your addiction? Maybe the habit has already taken a noticeable physical toll on your body. It's essential to take a step back and assess the potential harm your addiction may be causing to your physical health. By acknowledging the risks, you can make a conscious decision to take action toward a healthier and happier lifestyle.

My addictions put me at risk for, or have caused ____________________

____

Addictions can have a profound effect on our relationships with others. The impact can be significant, whether it's spending less time with family and friends or avoiding social events because they interfere with the addiction. Perhaps the addiction has caused you to withdraw from others, become irritable and moody, or even be abusive toward those around us, leading to strained or broken relationships. Maybe it's preventing you from pursuing new relationships or causing issues in existing ones. Whatever the case, addictions can harm our connections with others and make maintaining healthy relationships challenging. Therefore, it's crucial to take stock of how your addiction affects your interactions with others and seek help to overcome it.

What important moments or events have you missed out on because of your addiction?

I have missed out on ____

____

Who in your life has expressed concern about your behavior?

____

What steps can you take to repair any damage caused by your addiction and build stronger, healthier relationships?

I can start to repair damaged relationships by ______________________

____

____

Addictions can take a significant financial toll. Many addictions require ongoing purchases, such as cigarettes, alcohol, drugs, or unhealthy food. These expenses can quickly add up, leading to financial strain and potentially even debt. It can be difficult to fully realize the financial impact of an addiction until you take the time to add it up. Consider how much money you spend on your addiction each day, week, or month.

The amount I spend to feed my addiction is $__________ a day, $__________ a week, and $__________ per month.

Addictions can take a toll on your work life as well. It's common for addictions to impact job performance, leading to issues with productivity, attendance, and quality of work. The emotional and mental strain of addiction can also cause difficulties in the workplace, including conflicts with coworkers and management. Moreover, some habits can lead to legal issues that can result in losing a job or professional license. Therefore, it's essential to take a hard look at how your addiction affects your work and career aspirations. By seeking help and taking steps toward recovery, you can start to repair the damage and regain control over your professional life.

In what ways might your work possibly be affected or has been affected by your addiction?

My addiction has affected or may affect, my job by ____________________

____

Addictions can bring a range of minor but frustrating annoyances to our daily lives. For instance, if you're addicted to smoking, you might be tired of leaving your office and going out in the cold every time you need to light up. Or, if you can't resist the lure of fast food, you might be consistently late because you can't drive by a McDonald's without pulling through the drive-thru to get your French fry fix. These minor annoyances may seem insignificant, but they can add up and take a toll on our daily lives.

Reflect on the minor but persistent annoyances that your addiction brings to your daily life.

The annoyances of my addiction are ______________________________

____

How do they affect your work, relationships, and overall well-being?

The effects on my life are ______________________________

____

What specific actions can you take to start reducing the impact of these annoyances?

I can reduce these annoyances by ______________________________

____

2. **Positive changes you want in your life.** Let's get excited about the positive changes that will come once you let go of those pesky "peanuts"! Just imagine the sense of liberation and empowerment you'll feel once you break free from the chains of addiction. You'll have more time and money to invest in yourself and your passions.

Picture yourself achieving your wildest dreams and pursuing your true purpose without distractions or limitations. You'll feel more energized, confident, and proud of yourself than ever before. Not to mention, you'll be setting a fantastic example for those around you by making healthy choices and living your best life. So start brainstorming all the tremendous ways your life will improve once you let go of your "peanuts." Get excited about your future!

How will your life improve once you've let go of your addiction, the "peanuts" you have been holding onto?

The positive changes I wish to see in my life are ______________________

____

____

Finally, visualize your life post-addiction. Imagine the life you want after you let go of your addiction. See yourself feeling a sense of liberation you haven't experienced in years. Visualize having more time and resources to invest in the things that bring you joy, like spending time with loved ones or pursuing hobbies that make your heart sing. Envision yourself prioritizing your health and feeling the physical improvements that come with it. And don't forget about feeling proud and confident again. Creating a clear vision of your post-addiction life will keep you motivated to stay on track and make the changes necessary to achieve it.

In my new life, free from addictions, I am __________________________

____

____

____

____

____

____

____

____

3. **Commitment to quitting.** Let's face it—quitting anything can be challenging, especially when it's something you've been holding onto for a long time. But it's important to remember that your commitment to letting go of your "peanuts" will ultimately help you succeed. It's not easy, but it's worth it. Take the time to write down your solid reasons for quitting. Think about how your life will improve once you've let go of this addiction. Maybe you'll have more energy to pursue your passions or more money to travel the world. Perhaps you'll be able to repair relationships that were once strained because of your addiction. Whatever your reasons are, make sure they are genuine and important to you. The stronger your reasons are, the more likely you are to stay committed to your plan. So go ahead, write them down, and keep them somewhere visible as a reminder of why you're doing this.

I am letting go of ____________________ *because I deserve* ____________

____

____

____

4. **Set a date to quit.** Setting a date to quit is crucial, but don't be impulsive about it. Please don't set it for tomorrow unless you're certain that quitting cold turkey is your thing. Also, don't schedule it for more than a month from now, or you might lose your determination by then. Instead, aim for a date in the next few weeks, giving yourself enough time to become mentally and physically ready. Consider choosing a meaningful date to help motivate you, like your birthday, anniversary, or a significant event. Mark the day on your calendar and share it with your loved ones. Building up the anticipation will make you less likely to back down when the day arrives. Above all, make a firm commitment to yourself that you will quit by that date.

What is a significant date that you could choose to mark as your quitting day?

I commit to quit by (date) ________________________.

5. **Seek personal and professional support.** Quitting an addiction is tough; that is why having all the support you can get is essential. Think about it; even superheroes need sidekicks to help them save the world. Don't be afraid to ask for help! It's a sign of strength, not weakness. Do your research and find in-person or online support groups to help you through this challenging time. There are plenty of resources out there that are free, and the people involved are always welcoming and understanding. Make an appointment with a therapist that specializes in helping people overcome addictions. They have the expertise and training to provide the tools and techniques you need to succeed. Plus, you get to talk to someone who has seen and heard it all before without fear of judgment. And don't forget to lean on your friends and family for support. They care about you and want to see you succeed. Let them know what you're going through and ask them to respect your decision by not tempting you with the thing you're trying to quit.

Who are the people in your life that you can turn to for support during your journey to overcome addiction? Write down their names and how they can support you. Remember that it's okay to ask for help!

I will reach out to ____

____

6. **Slowly transition out of your addiction or quit "cold turkey."** Everyone is unique, and there's no one-size-fits-all approach to overcoming addiction. You get to decide what works best for you. Are you the type of person who can go "cold turkey" and never look back? Or do you need to gradually wean yourself off your "peanuts"

addiction? If you prefer the slow and steady approach, start by indulging less often and gradually reducing your dependence as your quit date approaches. Remind yourself that every small step is a step in the right direction.

Which approach do you think will work best for you? Are you ready to quit cold turkey, or do you need to take a more gradual process? Write down each approach's pros and cons and decide which feels most realistic and achievable for you.

Pros of quitting cold turkey ______________________________

____

Cons of quitting cold turkey ______________________________

____

Pros of quitting gradually ______________________________

____

Cons of quitting gradually ______________________________

____

Think of a time when you successfully broke a bad habit or addiction in the past. What approach did you use, and what did you learn from that experience? How can you apply those lessons to your current situation?

In the past ______________________________

____

Identify one minor change you can make today to start breaking your addiction. It could be as simple as cutting back on your "peanuts" intake or replacing one harmful habit with a positive one. Take that first step towards a healthier, happier life.

Today, I will ____

____

____

____

The journey to overcome addiction, to release your "peanuts," is a profound adventure within yourself. It's a testament to your resilience and strength. Remember, you don't have to face this journey alone. Seek the support of friends, family, and professionals who are ready to stand by your side. As you set your quit date and take those first steps, believe in yourself and the incredible future awaiting you. The road may be challenging, but the rewards of a healthier, happier, and addiction-free life are beyond measure. Embrace the adventure, for it leads to the discovery of your true self, free from the grip of addiction.

13

Uncovering Your Triggers

"Your triggers are your responsibility. It isn't the world's obligation to tiptoe around you."

-Anonymous

Navigating the Minefield

We all have unique triggers that tempt us to indulge in unhealthy habits. Once you know what situations, people, or emotions set off your addictive behaviors, you can develop strategies to deal with them. Stress is a common trigger for all types of addiction. Parties, social gatherings, specific situations, or even certain people can act as triggers. If stress triggers you, find healthy ways to manage stress, such as meditation, exercise, or journaling. If social gatherings or specific individuals trigger your addiction, create a plan before attending or interacting with them, such as bringing a sober friend or avoiding specific environments altogether. For example, if you can't resist milkshakes and French fries, passing by a fast-food drive-through on your way home could make you want to stop. If binge-eating while watching TV is your weakness, consider eating a healthy dinner before watching TV or taking a walk instead.

When it comes to food, take the opportunity to learn about your cravings. Mindfully savor each bite and ask yourself what you crave about the food. Is it the sauce, spices, seasonings, or texture? And ask yourself why you're craving it. Are you eating out of habit or feeding your emotions?

Can you find healthier food that satisfies the same craving? Don't punish yourself for giving in to food temptation. Instead, use it to identify your triggers and find healthier alternatives.

Triggers are not weaknesses. They're simply cues that your brain associates with your addiction. By recognizing and managing your triggers, you can gain more control over your addiction and live a happier, healthier life.

What are your triggers?

I know I am triggered to ____________________ *when* ______________

____

____

Write down a list of potential strategies to overcome your triggers. How can you plan to deal with your triggers in a healthy way?

I can overcome my triggers by ____________________________________

____

____

Dodging Distractions: Reclaim Your Space, Reclaim Your Focus

Listen, you've got to resist those distractions if you're going to kick your addiction to the curb. First things first, get rid of all those pesky reminders of your habit around the house, car, and workplace. You know, like that bottle of whiskey you have tucked away in the back of the cabinet, the ashtray you keep in your car for "emergencies," or the junk food stash hidden in your pantry. Instead, swap out those old items for things that make you feel good and encourage healthy choices. I'm talking fresh fruits and veggies in the fridge, a delightful book or two, and maybe even a nice potted plant to spruce up the living room. And if you're feeling extra motivated, why not redecorate your kitchen or rearrange your cupboards? It's all about changing your environment and starting fresh, my friend.

What items or objects in your environment remind you of your addiction?

The things that remind me of my addiction are ____________________

____

What changes can you make to remove those reminders in your home, car, or workplace?

I will ____

What positive items or decorations can you add to your environment to encourage healthy choices?

I can add ____

____

Limiting activities that serve as distractions is another way to help overcome addiction. Identify the activities that you often use as an excuse to indulge in your addiction and limit them. By limiting these distractions, you can create more time and energy to focus on healthy habits and activities that will help you overcome your addiction. Make a list of items or activities you already enjoy that can easily replace the addiction.

- o Walk around the block instead of a smoke break
- o Veggie burger instead of a greasy, fatty burger

- o Calming chamomile tea instead of an alcoholic drink
- o Extra veggies in place of French fries
- o ______________________________
- o ______________________________
- o ______________________________
- o ______________________________
- o ______________________________
- o ______________________________
- o ______________________________
- o ______________________________
- o ______________________________

Understanding and managing your triggers is a crucial step on the path to breaking free from addiction. These triggers, whether they're stress, specific situations, or emotional states, no longer have to control your actions. By identifying and preparing for them, you regain the power to make healthier choices. Remember, your triggers are not weaknesses—they're simply signals your brain associates with your addiction. Embrace the opportunity to learn from them, find healthier alternatives, and create an environment that supports your recovery. By resisting distractions and replacing old habits with positive choices, you're not just breaking free from addiction; you're embarking on a journey toward a more fulfilling and vibrant life.

14

Successfully Quitting and Surviving Withdrawal

"Real strength emerges not from what you can already do, but from conquering the obstacles you once believed were insurmountable."

-Anonymous

The Great Escape

It's time to make the great escape and emerge as a victor in your own life. Allow yourself to delve into the challenges and triumphs of breaking free from addictive patterns and navigating the turbulent waters of withdrawal. Whether you're seeking to quit a harmful habit, release toxic relationships, or release negative thought patterns, this section is your guide to finding liberation and reclaiming your power. Get ready to embark on a courageous journey of self-discovery, resilience, and personal growth as we explore the strategies, tools, and mindset shifts needed to overcome obstacles and emerge stronger on the other side.

Step One: Acknowledge Your Position - The Great Waking Up

Rise and shine, my friends! First things first, you must acknowledge that you are in the process of withdrawal. See it as your personal call to adventure, a divine tap on the shoulder from the Universe. Congratulate yourself on this! No, I'm not kidding. You're about to embark on the journey of self-discovery and healing. And guess what? You're the hero in this story. You are stronger than you think. Even Superman had to learn to fly.

Step Two: Acknowledge the Power of Intent - The GPS of Your Soul

Just like a GPS guides your car through uncharted territories, your intention will navigate you through this odyssey of withdrawal. Set your intention solid and clear. Remember that it's not about 'I should' or 'I need to,' but 'I choose to.' This is your journey, your life. So embrace your inner Captain Kirk and boldly go where you've never been before!

Write about a time you set a clear intention and achieved it. How did it feel? How can you channel that same energy and determination into your withdrawal journey?

___

___

___

___

___

___

___

Step Three: Self-Care - Be Your Own Best Friend

Withdrawal is a demanding journey, akin to climbing Mount Everest without the right gear. Self-care is the oxygen tank you need to reach the summit. Listen to your body, take care of your needs, and don't forget to pamper yourself a bit. Give your body what it needs—healthy food, plenty of rest, and oodles of water. Practice mindfulness or meditation. Become your own best friend. After all, if you can't be your own best friend, who else will?

Imagine yourself as your own best friend. What advice would you give yourself? How would you comfort and care for yourself during this challenging time?

As my own best friend, I can healthily comfort myself by ________________

____

____

____

____

Step Four: Exercise - Your Personal Energizer Bunny

Remember those Energizer Bunny commercials? It just keeps going and going and going … Well, that's you with exercise! It's not about bench-pressing a small car or running a marathon (unless you want to, in which case, go you!). A brisk walk, yoga, or even dancing to your favorite tunes can fill you with energy, release feel-good hormones, and help you combat withdrawal symptoms. So move that fabulous body of yours!

Describe a form of exercise that makes you feel invigorated and powerful. How can you incorporate this activity into your daily routine?

Exercises that make me feel alive are ______________________________

____

I can incorporate this exercise into my daily routine by ________________

____

Step Five: The Miracle of Patience - The Turtle's Secret

Every journey has its speed bumps, and withdrawal is no different. It's not a race. Embody the wisdom of the turtle. Take slow, steady steps. Patience is not about waiting but keeping a good attitude while working hard. The miracle isn't that you finished but had the courage to start. Embrace the power of patience, and remember that, as the turtle says, "slow and steady wins the race." Trust in the process and keep moving forward, one step at a time.

Reflect on a time when patience paid off for you. Can you draw parallels between that experience and your current journey? How can the wisdom of the turtle inspire you in this process?

My patience paid off in the past when I ______________________________

____

____

The wisdom of the turtle inspires me to ______________________________

____

____

Step Six: The Power of Positivity - Your Tribe Awaits

Positivity is contagious, and it's time you caught that bug! It's the uplifting notes you leave for yourself on the fridge, the inspiring podcasts you listen to, and the motivational biographies you read. Positivity is your secret weapon, safety net, and personal cheerleading squad.

Surround yourself with cheerleaders, not naysayers. This is your tribe, people who uplift, motivate, and believe in you, even when you find it hard to believe in yourself. Positivity is not about ignoring life's difficulties but about overcoming them. Remember that positive energy is contagious. But be careful; so is the negative. Choose wisely.

Write a letter to your future self filled with words of encouragement and hope.

____

____

____

____

____

____

____

List five positive affirmations to repeat to yourself every day.

1. ____
2. ____
3. ____
4. ____
5. ____

Step Seven: Keep Clear of Triggers - Dodging Landmines

This journey is about knowing your battlefield. Be on the lookout for triggers that might lure you back to old habits. Recognize your triggers and stay clear. It's like dodging landmines on your path, not because you fear them, but because you value your journey too much to let anything derail it.

Identify your triggers and write about strategies you can use to avoid them. How can you turn those moments of potential weakness into strength?

____

____

____

____

Step Eight: Don't Give in to Rationalization - The Sirens' Song

Rationalization is the siren's song, tempting you off course. Beware the siren's song of rationalization that tries to coax you back into the clutches of your old habits. It's that voice saying, "Just one more time won't hurt." But you know what? You're smarter than that. You can see through its disguise. You're the captain of your ship, and you have the power to steer clear of these temptations. Every rationalization is just a diversion from your chosen path. So plug your ears, stay on your course, and adventure on!

Recall a moment when you didn't give in to rationalization. What strength did you draw upon then?

The strengths I have drawn upon in the past are ____________________

How can you tap into that strength now?

I can tap into this strength by ____________________________

____

____

Step Nine: Don't Let Relapse Be the End of Your Journey - The Comeback Story

Relapse isn't a dead-end; it's a detour. It's not the villain in your story; it's the plot twist that makes your comeback even more glorious. If you relapse, it's not a failure but a learning opportunity, a chance to come back stronger, wiser, and with a few more tricks up your sleeve. Remember that falling is not failing; failing is not getting up again. Your journey is not defined by your falls but by your comebacks!

Write about a setback you've experienced and how you overcame it. How did that experience shape you, and how can it provide insight for managing potential relapses?

I overcame a setback when ________________________________

____

____

____

*This setback shaped me and provided insight by*________________________

____

Step Ten: Celebrate Your Progress - You're Doing It!

Last but not least, celebrate your progress! Every step you take towards overcoming withdrawal, no matter how small, is a victory. So don't be shy to do a little dance, make a little love, and celebrate! Or simply pat yourself on the back. Know that you are a powerful, magnificent being on a path toward healing and recovery. You can do this. After all, you're the hero of this story. Now, go out there and shine!

Imagine it's a year from now, and you've successfully managed your withdrawal. Describe in detail how you would celebrate this achievement. What does it look like, sound like, and feel like?

A year from now, I will celebrate my success by ______________________

____

____

____

As you move forward, remember that you are the hero of your own story, and you have the power to shape your destiny. Embrace the challenges and triumphs that come your way, for they are the building blocks of your transformation. Set clear intentions, practice self-care, exercise your body, and cultivate patience while surrounding yourself with positivity and a supportive tribe.

Stay vigilant against triggers and the siren's song of rationalization. Know that setbacks are not failures—they are opportunities to learn and grow stronger. Celebrate every small victory along the way, for each step brings you closer to the radiant, addiction-free life you deserve.

You are doing it! Your journey is a beacon of hope and inspiration for others facing similar challenges. So, keep shining, keep moving forward, and keep embracing the adventure of you!

15

Discovery of you

"Love yourself...
enough to take the actions required for your happiness ...
enough to cut yourself loose from the drama-filled past ...
enough to set a high standard for relationships ...
enough to feed your mind and body in a healthy manner ...
enough to forgive yourself...
enough to move on."

-Unknown

Dive into Your Depths

Genuine healing occurs when you allow yourself permission to look at whatever feelings live below the triggers, learn from them, release them, and grow.

Embrace a profound affection for the person you are. Accept it or not, you're the one constant companion in your life's journey, so it's high time to halt the self-sabotage, dive headfirst into self-love, and discover the marvel that is you! You have every right and deserve the life of your dreams. It's your cosmic inheritance to lead an extraordinary, tranquil, and healthy existence. So gear up to delve deep, confront your self-limiting beliefs, and discover your authentic power and truth.

Ask yourself—"Do I love myself?"

How do you perceive the concept of questioning your self-love?

The thoughts I harbor toward self-love encompass ______________________

____

The emotions I associate with loving myself are ______________________

____

Self vs. Others: A Journey Beyond Comparison

"The fastest way to kill something special is to compare it to something else."

Listen closely, my friend; you are an extraordinary, one-of-a-kind creation of the cosmos! Imagine if you'd never heard a single note sung by another—wouldn't your voice be the sweetest melody you'd ever heard? But alas, we live in a world of photoshopped magazine covers, cosmetic surgeries, and seemingly flawless lives displayed on Facebook and Instagram. It's easy to feel like an imperfect puzzle piece in this airbrushed picture.

What, or who, are you constantly measuring yourself against?

My comparisons often involve ______________________________

____

What about them makes you feel less than the masterpiece you truly are?

The things about them that cast a shadow on my perfection are ___________

____

____

How does this affect your self-esteem?

My self-worth in light of these comparisons appears as ________________

____

____

What untruths are entangled in this comparison?

When I compare myself to them, I encounter fabrications such as ________

____

____

There's absolutely no cause for guilt or shame if you find yourself gauging your worth against someone else's. Comparisons are simply your mind's way of assessing your progress, but remember that they often distort the truth more than they reveal it. You have not trod in another's footsteps, just as no one has trod in yours. So diminish the relevance of comparison by living your life according to your terms. Cease the comparisons, cherish your innate talents, and recognize the truth of your unique identity.

Consider this—If you could engage in anything without drawing comparisons, what would it be?

*Freed from the shackles of comparison, I would passionately*____________

____

____

Now, muster the courage to transcend your fears and take that action. Seize the opportunity, discover a safe haven, belt out your favorite song, dance as if no one's watching, purchase that bikini, look yourself in the mirror, and affirm, "I am beautiful" … Whatever it may be, engage in it knowing that you're incredible and that only you can do it in your unique way!

What was the sensation of liberating yourself from comparison and embracing your authentic self?

*When I engage in an activity purely as myself, I feel*____________________

____

____

List at least nine attributes that you love about your unparalleled self.

1. ____
2. ____
3. ____
4. ____
5. ____
6. ____
7. ____
8. ____
9. ____

Embracing the truth that you can't feel lonely if you enjoy the company of the person you're alone with—is the key to a fulfilling journey. It's an invitation to appreciate your own unique melody in the symphony of life. When you genuinely admire who you are, solitude transforms from a state of loneliness into an oasis of self-discovery and reflection. So cherish your individuality, let your unique song reverberate throughout your journey, and dance to the beat of your own drum joyfully in the rhythm of self-love and acceptance.

Beliefs: The Silent Puppeteers of Life

"Believe nothing, no matter where you read it or who has said, not even if I have said it, unless it agrees with your own reason and your own common sense."
-Buddha

Perfection, my friend, is being unapologetically you. You are here to be yourself, not a carbon copy of someone else or a puppet dancing to another's tune. So many of us are handed an invisible compass by our parents or those who raised us. This compass is set to direct us toward their values, beliefs, and judgments. But, like a compass that points to a long-abandoned treasure, these can mislead. They may falter or lose their way. It's your task to outgrow that compass and chart your course by the stars.

Have any authority figures—perhaps a religious leader, parent, or teacher—dictated how you should live and what you should believe? What are their expectations of you?

The voices guiding my beliefs and actions include ____________________

____

____

The beliefs they've instilled in me are ____________________

____

____

Their expectations for me include ____________________

____

____

Do you notice a transformation in yourself when you're in their company? How do you change in their presence?

I morph into a different version of myself by ______________________

____

____

How does this differ from who you truly are?

The ways this persona differs from my authentic self include ____________

____

____

Deep within, your truth and beliefs hum their own unique tune. Spend some quiet time alone, listen closely, and trust your inner compass. Grant yourself the freedom to wander off the path others have dictated. Abandon that old compass, let the stars illuminate your journey, and follow their glow home.

What whispers is your inner guide sharing with you?

My inner voice whispers ______________________________

____

____

Is your truth a different melody than what others have sung to you? How does it differ?

My truth strays from the familiar tune in ways such as ______________

____

____

What strategies can you employ to peacefully live the life you were destined for while maintaining respect and good relationships with those who might disagree?

I can keep my authenticity and harmonious relationships by ____________

____

____

The Five-Perspective Journey to Discover Your Truth

Welcome to a journey of self-discovery and introspection. This is no ordinary adventure but a profoundly personal exploration that will traverse the landscapes of your inner world, from your individual perspective to those of a counselor, spiritual guide, great teacher, and even the divine. It's a sacred expedition of self-awareness, where you'll delve into the depths of your heart and soul, uncovering truths and insights that have, until now, remained hidden. This journey requires courage, for it will challenge you to strip away the layers of external influence and listen to the voice within. So take a deep breath, open your heart, and embark on this exciting adventure to discover your truth.

You can embark on this journey through spoken word or by recording your thoughts in the spaces provided.

Begin by asking yourself: What question is resonating within your heart?

First Stop: Your Perspective

Close your eyes and take nine deep, rejuvenating breaths.

Now, let your thoughts flow freely. What are your queries?

What fears, emotions, and concerns are tied to these queries?

Once you feel you've offloaded your thoughts, take a momentary pause, rise, and shake off any lingering tension.

Second Stop: The Counselor's Perspective

Shift your awareness to that of a counselor, a sage advisor, or an objective third party well-versed in your question.

Close your eyes and take nine deep breaths as you transition into the counselor's shoes. What would a counselor make of your query?

In what ways does this viewpoint differ from your initial perspective?

How does this new lens of understanding feel?

Once you're satisfied with the counselor's viewpoint, take a breather, stand, and stroll around.

Third Stop: The spiritual guide's Perspective

Direct your focus toward a spiritual guide, your higher self, or a guardian angel. Close your eyes, breathe deeply nine times, and step into the viewpoint of the spiritual guide.

From this vantage point, reflect upon the earlier perspectives. What fresh insights do you glean from this elevated viewpoint?

____

____

What higher truth does it reveal?

____

____

When you're done exploring the spiritual guide's perspective, take a short rest, stand, and stretch your legs.

Fourth Stop: The Great Teacher's Perspective

Position your consciousness in the shoes of a revered teacher like Jesus, Buddha, Muhammad, St. Francis, Mother Theresa, or Confucius.

Close your eyes, take nine deep breaths, and assume the mindset of your chosen teacher. From their viewpoint, you can glimpse across the vast expanse of human history and the world. So trust your intuition and seek the broader narrative behind your question.

Place your hands on your heart and tune into this great teacher's message of truth and inspiration.

What wisdom have you gained?

___

___

After you're done with this viewpoint, take a moment to rest.

Fifth Stop: God's Perspective

Tap into the energy that you connect with as God. Close your eyes, take nine deep breaths, and align with divine consciousness.

From this viewpoint, you'll see that all is love, everything and everyone is interconnected, and everything has a purpose. Everything is unfolding in perfect order, just as it should. Place your hands over your heart and receive divine wisdom.

What truths have been revealed to you?

___

___

___

What is the highest purpose?

___

___

___

Once you're done, take a short break.

Final Stop: Your Perspective

Return to your own self. Place your hands over your heart and take several deep breaths as you assimilate everything you have learned.

What new insights and wisdom have you received?

___

___

___

What is the answer to your initial question?

___

___

___

How do you feel now?

___

___

___

Congratulations! You've completed a significant journey, traversing various perspectives, and exploring the depths of your being. The insights and truths you've uncovered are precious gems of wisdom unique to your personal journey. This journey doesn't end here. The landscapes of your inner world are vast, and there are still many uncharted territories to explore. As you continue your adventure, may you always listen to your heart, trust your intuition, and let your authentic truth guide your way. You have embarked on the most beautiful journey—the journey to self-discovery and truth. Keep exploring, keep growing, and most importantly, keep being you.

Cultivating Self-Worth: A Journey to Unleashing Deservability

"What if you could love yourself so profoundly that your happiness became your top priority? Life itself supports your well-being, urging you to care for yourself. Embrace self-love deeply, and the universe will reflect your value, inviting a lifetime of fulfillment from within."
- Alan Cohen

Deservability and self-worth are two essential ingredients for living a life of joy and abundance. Do you ever catch yourself thinking you don't deserve the good things in life? Perhaps you must work harder or measure up to someone's standard to be worthy. Has your internal chatterbox convinced you that you're not worthy of something spectacular? Have a little chat with yourself and investigate where these limiting beliefs come from.

What's the script of self-restriction you've been rehearsing in your head?

The lines I've been rehearsing about my not being deserving are __________

____

What goodies have you convinced yourself you're not deserving of?

I've convinced myself I'm not worthy of ______________________________

____

Why do you feel that way?

I feel undeserving because ________________________________

____

____

Who handed you this script of unworthiness and non-deserving?

The playwrights of my unworthiness saga are ____________________

____

Here's the truth—the only thing you don't deserve is to keep listening to the nonsense, chaos, and bull hockey you've been telling yourself. Are you ready to drop the script and pick up a new one? What tales of unworthiness or non-deserving will you toss into the trash bin?

I'm ready to toss the tales of ______________________________

____

____

What beautiful things do you deserve in pursuing a happy, healthy life?
I deserve a life abundant with _____________________________

____

____

You see, you deserve to take that bag of self-deprecating talk that's been weighing you down and give it a new job. Think of it as a bag of manure (stick with me here!). Yes, it stinks, but it can be useful. It's time to take that bag and spread it over the garden of your mind, turning those pungent thoughts into fertilizer for new, beautiful growth within you. So are you ready to plant the seeds of a growth mindset and nurture them with a dose of positivity?

Instead of thinking (Limited mindset)	**Think (Growth mindset)**
I am a failure.	*I am creating a new lifestyle, it won't always be perfect, but I can do better.*
I don't deserve to be happy.	*It is my birthright to live a happy life.*

Take a moment to embark on a journey through your life story. Pack your bag of memories and jump on the magic carpet of retrospection. Start with the dawn of your existence, your childhood. Chronicle the rollercoaster ride of your life, the peaks and valleys, your secret thoughts and steadfast beliefs, your trials, and your triumphs. What's the tale that has sculpted the magnificent masterpiece that you are today?

My journey started ______________________________

As your quill danced across the parchment of your past, did you stumble upon any dark chapters? Any haunting echoes of suffering that you've shoved in the dusty corners of your mind but now realize it's time to release them? What are these daunting shadows you're ready to shed?

The experiences I am ready to release ______________________________

____

____

What wisdom can you learn from these encounters?

Reflecting on these experiences, I have learned ______________________

____

How can they pave the way towards forgiveness and release?

Forgiveness is a gift I give myself—a release, a renewal. By forgiving, I am releasing ____

____

____

____

____

Now, find a photograph of yourself as a young sprout. Gaze into the eyes of the fledgling you once were and engage in a heart-to-heart conversation. Then, ask your pint-sized self the following questions:

- What tickles your joy buds?
- How can I nourish this joy?
- What dreams fill your nights?

- What sends shivers down your spine?
- How can I help you feel safe and sound?
- What do you want to whisper in my ear?

What heartfelt message do you want to send to your younger self?

Next, take a detour to the mirror and engage in a heart-to-heart dyad with the person staring back at you. Share with yourself the blueprint you've sketched for a joyous, healthy life. Express how immensely proud you are of every battle you've fought and every victory you've savored.

And then, gaze deep into your own eyes and say the magic words— "I love you."

Carve out some time to journal about your heartfelt exchange with your reflection. Feel free to pour out every emotion, every revelation, and every flutter in your heart as you say those three beautiful words to yourself.

Within you lies a treasure of everything you need to live the spectacular, serene, healthy life you yearn for. You, my friend, are a universe in yourself, waiting to be explored.

____

____

____

____

____

____

____

____

____

____

____

____

____

You, my friend, are a universe in yourself, waiting to be explored. As you reflect on your journey, release the burdens of unworthiness, and cultivate self-love and self-compassion, remember that you are deserving of all the beauty and joy life has to offer. The script of self-restriction can be replaced with a narrative of growth and abundance. Your past experiences, both light and shadow, hold valuable lessons that can pave the way to forgiveness and release. Embrace the sprout of joy within you, nourish your dreams, and whisper words of love to your inner child. You have the power to create a life that honors your worth and celebrates your unique journey. So, with an open heart, step boldly into the adventure of you and let your inner universe shine.

16

Freedom of Forgiveness

"I forgive and set myself free."

-Unknown

Breaking Chains of the Past

Peace of mind, my dear friend, is a priceless gem, and the act of forgiveness is the key to its treasure chest. When we forgive, we exchange a life of resentment and bitterness for a life of freedom. Imagine every betrayal or hurt like a snakebite. Even after the wound heals, the venom—a toxic blend of anger and hatred—remains, coursing through your veins. The damage is done; the snake can't un-bite you. While the snake may have long moved on, uncaring of its bite, the lingering venom is what truly harms you—robbing your peace of mind.

The antidote? Let go and cleanse yourself of the venom of the past. Relegate your memories to the realm of 'what has been,' free from emotional shackles. Refrain from punishing yourself over past events and grant yourself the liberty to find peace in the present.

Remember that everyone from your past acted based on their own circumstances and understanding. They did what they did, and you can't ask for more. Seek out the hidden lessons in your experiences, and when you appreciate these lessons, you'll find the pain ebbing away. When you no longer ache, you'll know you've truly released your past—that, my friend, is the essence of forgiveness. As the saying goes, I will forgive their iniquity and remember their sin no more.

Consider forgiveness as your personal antidote, a miraculous potion that neutralizes the poison you've let circulate within you. With forgiveness, the venom loses its deadly sting.

What poisonous memories are you ready to neutralize with forgiveness in your life?

I'm prepared to neutralize and forgive ______________________

____

What silver linings have emerged from these dark clouds?

From these dark clouds, silver linings have emerged in the form of ________

____

____

What valuable lessons have your past experiences taught you?

My past experiences have gifted me with lessons like ______________

____

____

Observe your emotional responses. How ready are you to let go on a scale of 1-10? ________

If you're not quite at a ten, what beliefs are holding you back from forgiving and releasing?

The beliefs anchoring me and obstructing my path to forgiveness are

____

____

How do you plan to release these bitter memories, forgive their iniquity, and remember their sin no more?

To fully release the past and forgive, I will ______________________________

____

____

As you embark on this extraordinary journey of forgiveness, remember the stars in the sky were formed from great turmoil and chaos, yet they shine beautifully, unapologetically. Just like them, you've been through your share of cosmic turbulence, but it's all in the past, and the light of your forgiveness is your beacon forward. The universe doesn't hold grudges, and neither should you. So here's to you, my dear friend—the forgiving, the glowing, the ever-evolving being of light. Let the venom be neutralized, let the wounds heal, and let your light shine brighter. Because, at the end of the day, you're not just stardust—you're a darn shooting star, blazing a trail toward an unburdened future of peace and serenity. So forgive, let go, and never stop shining!

Forgiveness Affirmations

Ah, affirmations! The linguistic ladders that let us climb out of our self-dug pits of resentment and into the glorious sunshine of forgiveness.

Please practice these forgiveness affirmations at least twice daily until you feel entirely forgiven and at ease. Say each affirmation three times, then place your hand over your heart and take several deep, heartfelt breaths.

Forgive Others

"I fully and freely forgive and release now. I forgive everyone, everything, and every experience, past or present, that deserves forgiveness now. I positively forgive everyone."

Forgive Self

"I am now forgiven by everyone and everything that deserves to forgive me, past or present. I am now positively forgiven by everyone. All is forgiven and released now."

Forgiveness isn't just a word; it's a deep, cleansing breath that expels the stale air of past grudges and fills your lungs with the fresh oxygen of peace. With each affirmation, take those deep, heartfelt breaths. Let them be the wind beneath your wings as you soar into a future unburdened by the past.

17

Emotional Alchemy

"Despite life's challenges, we retain the ultimate freedom to shape our attitude and choose our own path. When circumstances are beyond our control, we face the invitation to transform ourselves."

-Victor Frankl

Transmuting Stress, Emotions, and Trauma

"No person, place, or thing has any power over me. I am free." This is a mantra to live by when it comes to emotions and stress. Let's start with a riddle—What can surge like a tidal wave, remain still as a pond, yet never move from its place? The answer—Emotion. It's Energy in Motion. You, my friend, are the superhero of your adventure. You decide how you feel about your life experiences. The energy from these experiences manifests as emotions; your reaction to those emotions is what we commonly call "stress."

Have you ever been caught red-handed blaming the universe for your emotions and stress? We've all been there. "It's his fault I'm stressed," or "She made me eat that entire cheesecake, and now I'm on a guilt trip." And let's not even start on how we're convinced only we can do things right. But here's a secret—holding onto negative emotions, grudges, and stress is like doing the cha-cha with a bag of bricks strapped to your back. It's exhausting; before you know it, you're out of step with life. If you're constantly feeling like you're under the weather or that stubborn weight just won't budge, it's time to shed those heavy emotions and stress that are weighing you down.

I remember when I discovered I had breast cancer. I felt like I had been strapped into an emotional roller coaster, unsure of what tomorrow would bring or if I even had a tomorrow to live for. But amidst the tumultuous ride, I found the strength to work through my emotions, let go of the fear, and trust in the outcome's flow and perfection.

Remember that no person, place, or thing has any power over you. Only you have the power to turn on the 'stress' switch. It's time to take back the reins and ride into the sunset of emotional freedom.

Emotions, you see, are the fuel propelling our thoughts. Like electricity completing a circuit, our emotions trigger neurons to release specific biochemicals. In other words, your thought patterns are the conductors, your emotions are the orchestra, and your body is the audience experiencing the symphony. The good news? You're the maestro! You decide the rhythm and pace.

When facing a serious illness, it's easy to let fear grab the conductor's baton. But remember, your power isn't in an uncertain future but in the NOW. So practice letting go of fear. Change your tune from feeling helpless to trusting in your healing abilities.

Let's strike up a new melody by asking ourselves some thought-provoking questions. Bring your awareness to what needs to be addressed, changes you need to make, and any faulty thinking you need to toss out like a sour note. Once you've done this, you've taken the first step toward self-empowerment rather than remaining the victim.

What stress or emotion are you dealing with now?

The current stress or emotion that I'm grappling with is ________________

____

Where did that emotion or stress originate?

*The origin of this emotion or stress can be traced back to*________________

____

How has it emotionally or physically affected you?

This particular emotion or stress has impacted me in the following ways (emotionally/physically):

____

____

Has it altered any relationships?

Yes/No, it has altered my relationships. The relationships that have been affected include ____

____

____

How have these relationships been affected?

The impact on these relationships has manifested in the following ways:

____

____

Because of these effects, how do you behave differently than you would otherwise?

Due to these effects, I've noticed changes in my behavior. For instance, I now

____

____

What are you learning from being conscious of how emotions and stress affect you?

By being conscious of how emotions and stress affect me, I'm learning that

____

____

How can you create more positive emotions and outcomes from similar situations in the future?

To create more positive emotions and outcomes from similar situations in the future, I will ____

____

____

How will these ideas serve you?

These ideas will serve me in my journey towards emotional well-being by

____

____

____

Alchemy of the Soul

Rumi once shared a profound insight, "I saw grief drinking a cup of sorrow and called out, 'It tastes sweet, does it not?' 'You've caught me,' grief answered, 'and you've ruined my business. How can I sell sorrow when you know it's a blessing?'"

This, my dear friend, is the roadmap to our life journey. The mind and body are fellow travelers, trekking through the landscapes of our existence. When we let trauma, stress, and emotions hitch a ride, they don't just sit quietly in the backseat; they seep into our very cells and leave imprints that can cause physical discomfort and disease.

But we're in the driver's seat! So it's time to steer clear of these heavy burdens and cruise toward the horizon of healing.

First, tune into your emotional GPS, and trace the route of your stress and trauma and their physical footprints. For example, whenever you set foot in your mother-in-law's house, your shoulders morph into bricks, or your lower back aches.

What stress, emotions, or trauma are you holding on to?

I am holding onto ______________________________________

____

____

How do these burdens show up in your body?

They show up in my body in the form of ____________________

____

____

The next leg of our healing journey is to navigate away from these blockages, transmute them, and ultimately turn them into landmarks of blessings. I'll share with you two pathways that helped me during my healing quest. Choose to do one or both and allow some time to journal afterward. Repeat as often as desired to steer clear of the chaos in your life.

The Healing Bubble: A Journey of Emotional Release

1. Close your eyes, take a deep breath, and embark on a journey within yourself. Picture a bubble as large as your own body emerging from the depths of your imagination. You're about to enter this bubble, your very own sanctuary of transformation.
2. Step inside this bubble, your personal space of healing. Pay attention to the discomfort within your body, the spots where stress, emotions, and trauma have taken root.
3. Visualize the energy trapped in these pain points. It's time to set this energy free. Imagine it exploding out of your body, filling the bubble around you. Shake it off, push it out, and release it with all your might! Allow yourself to let go of this pent-up negative energy. Feel the freedom as you let go, and the weight of these burdens decrease.
4. When you feel the bubble is saturated with this released energy, step outside, leaving the bubble behind. Then, close the bubble quickly, trapping the negative energy inside.
5. Look at this bubble, this sphere of your past discomfort. Assign it a name, give it a color – externalize it, separate it from your essence.
6. Now, visualize yourself enveloped by a clear, bright, white light—a cocoon of purity and positivity. Place your hand over your heart, taking several deep, heartfelt breaths. Each breath draws in the white light, filling you with a sense of peace and tranquility.
7. Repeat this process at least once more, ensuring you have dispelled all the negative energy. When you step out of the bubble for the last time, bask in the white light around you, taking a few more calming breaths.
8. Feeling complete, it's time to send the bubble on its journey. Kick it upwards, imagining it soaring through the roof, beyond the

clouds, higher and higher into space. See its journey towards the sun, with its flaming heat incinerating all the negativity within.

9. Watch as the bubble transforms into a sphere of pure, brilliant, white light. Witness it exploding into a million fragments of sparkling light, slowly descending back to earth, showering you with a sense of calm and serenity.
10. Take a moment to journal your experience, imprinting this journey of release and renewal into your consciousness. This exercise is about releasing your issues, acknowledging them, processing them, and finding strength in their release. You are strong, you are capable, and you are on a journey to greater emotional freedom.

Embrace the Flow: A Process to Release Emotions

1. Take a moment to center yourself and place your hand gently on your chest. Choose an emotion you wish to release and assign it a color.
2. Visualize your hand as a powerful magnet, drawing this colored emotion from within you. Allow the emotion to flow like a river into your hand, its color becoming more vibrant with each passing moment.
3. Focus on your hand, feeling its magnetic pull. As the heat in your hand increases, you are releasing emotions; if your hand tingles, you are releasing thoughts. Connect with the feeling, envisioning it as the color, and let it flow freely.
4. Relax and take several deep breaths. Feel the heat or tingling in your hands subside while the color of the flow becomes softer and lighter. Continue until you experience a sense of release and peace.
5. Repeat the affirmation nine times with your hand still on your chest— "Love and peace flow through my hands and throughout my whole being now."
6. Once complete, shake off the residual energy from your hands. Rinse them with saltwater or cold water, symbolically washing away the emotion you released.
7. Finally, journal your experience, capturing the essence of your emotional release. This process is a testament to your inner strength and resilience as you consciously work towards greater emotional freedom and well-being.

___

___

___

____

____

____

____

____

____

____

Emotion, as we've learned, is truly energy in motion. It surges and stills, but its power lies in our hands. You have the ability to choose your responses, to transmute stress and emotions into opportunities for growth and healing.

Remember that you are the alchemist of your own emotions. You have the power to shape your attitude and choose your path, even in the face of life's challenges. Embrace this power, and let it guide you toward a life filled with emotional freedom, well-being, and the joy of transformation. Your adventure continues, and the path ahead is illuminated by the brilliance of your inner light.

18

Mind-Body Connection

"The body is the servant of the mind. It obeys the operations of the mind, whether they be deliberately chosen or automatically expressed."

- James Allen

Mindful Transcendence

Have you ever observed the profound connection between your mind and your body? It's fascinating how the thoughts in our mind can influence the sensations and responses in our physical body and vice versa. Take a moment now to explore this mind-body connection through a simple exercise known as the Lemon Exercise.

Find a comfortable seat, ensuring your spine is straight, and your body is relaxed. Rest your hands gently in your lap. If it feels comfortable, close your eyes to enhance your focus and immersion in the exercise.

Now, let your imagination take you to your kitchen table. Visualize a vibrant, ripe lemon placed right in front of you. Take a moment to picture the lemon in your mind, noticing its color, texture, and shape. As you continue the exercise, fully engage your senses to experience the mind-body connection.

Imagine reaching out and picking up the lemon. Feel its weight in your hand and notice the cool sensation of its surface against your skin. Next, visualize yourself taking a knife and carefully cutting the lemon in half, releasing its refreshing aroma.

Hold half the lemon in your hand and bring it closer to your nose.

Then, in your mind's eye, inhale deeply and imagine the scent of the lemon filling your nostrils. Notice how your body might respond to the imagined smell, perhaps activating your salivary glands or creating a subtle tingling sensation.

Finally, take a virtual bite of the lemon. Feel the texture of the juicy flesh on your teeth and tongue. Allow yourself to fully experience the tangy, sour, or refreshing taste. Pay attention to any physical responses that arise in your body as you vividly imagine biting into the lemon.

Take a moment to reflect on your experience during the Lemon Exercise. What did you notice? Did you feel a tingling in your mouth or a subtle change in your salivation? Did your body respond in any way to the visualization of biting into the lemon? Reflect on the connection between your mind and your body during this exercise. How did your thoughts and imagination influence the physical sensations and responses in your body?

By imagining the lemon, the following sensations showed up in my physical body: ____

____

By engaging in this exercise, you've witnessed firsthand how the power of your thoughts and imagination can influence your body's physical sensations and responses. This mind-body connection profoundly reminds us of the interplay between our thoughts, emotions, and physical experiences.

Consider a time when you have felt strong emotions, such as excitement, fear, or sadness. How did those emotions manifest in your body? Did you notice any physical sensations or changes?

When I feel strong emotions, my body seems to react by ________________

____

____

Think about a situation where you experienced a shift in your body's sensations, such as feeling tension or relaxation. How did that affect your thoughts and emotions?

When my body relaxed, my thoughts and emotions were those of __________

____

____

Embrace the profound connection between your thoughts, emotions, and physical sensations, and discover the power of nurturing a harmonious relationship between your mind and body.

As we explore the fascinating interplay between the mind and body, let's transition from the vivid imagery of the lemon exercise to the broader concept of healing the mind and body. Just like the tangy taste of lemon can stimulate our senses and evoke physical sensations, it serves as a reminder of the profound connection between our thoughts, emotions, and physical well-being. By recognizing that our experiences, beliefs, and emotions can affect our body's energetic balance, we open ourselves to the possibility of deeper healing and self-discovery.

Exploring the interconnectedness between our mind, emotions, and physical well-being is fascinating. While some bodily issues may be attributed to external factors like diet or movement, it's equally important to consider the influence of our state of mind and emotions on our overall physicality. Like a complex electrical system, our body operates based on the flow of energy through its pathways, often referred to as meridian points in ancient Chinese medicine.

Think of it this way—our thoughts, emotions, and bodies are all intricately intertwined forms of energy. It might sound a bit out there, but when you delve deeper, it becomes clear how our experiences, emotions, and beliefs can become energetically stored within the body. Every disease or ailment may not have a direct emotional cause. Still, each instance of illness or pain serves as an opportunity for us to explore the deeper layers of our being, uncovering the profound connection between our mind and body.

A few years ago, my world was shaken to its core when a cancer diagnosis came crashing into my life like a fierce storm. It hit me with such force that it seemed as if the ground beneath me had crumbled away, leaving me consumed by a whirlwind of emotions. Fear of the unknown gripped my heart, and I couldn't help but feel a deep frustration with myself for not recognizing the insidious presence that had taken root within me.

In the midst of this storm, I sought solace in the quiet moments of meditation. A profound realization washed over me as I allowed myself to sink into the depths of stillness. I discovered the cancer had chosen to reside in my left breast, closely above my heart. It served as a poignant reminder, urging me to open my heart and love in the face of adversity.

I began to understand that this cancer was not merely a physical ailment but a symbolic representation of the barriers I had built around my heart. It was a wake-up call, urging me to examine the depths of my being and how I approached life. I realized that I had unknowingly closed myself off from the love within me and the love surrounding me.

With this newfound awareness, I embarked on a journey of self-discovery and healing. I delved into the depths of my heart, unraveling the layers of fear, doubt, and self-limiting beliefs that had constricted me for so long. I gradually opened myself up to the transformative power of love through meditation and mindfulness practices.

As I nurtured the flame within my heart, I felt its warmth spread throughout my entire being. It became a beacon of hope and resilience, guiding me through the darkest times. I realized that love was not only a force of healing but also a catalyst for growth and transformation.

In the face of cancer, I consciously chose to love and accept myself unconditionally. I released the burden of self-blame and embraced the belief that I deserved love and compassion, regardless of my circumstances. This shift in perspective allowed me to see cancer not as a malicious enemy but as a messenger, offering me an opportunity to deepen my connection with myself and the world around me.

With each passing day, I learned to dance with cancer, weaving love, and acceptance into every step. I understood that healing was not just about eradicating disease from my body but also about cultivating a harmonious relationship between my mind, body, and spirit. I nurtured my body with nourishing foods, surrounded myself with a supportive community, and practiced self-care rituals that replenished my soul.

Through this journey, I discovered the power of self-love and compassion. I learned to listen to the whispers of my heart, honoring its desires and needs. As I opened myself up to love, I realized that love was the ultimate healer for my body and my entire being.

Today, as I reflect upon my journey, I am filled with gratitude for the cancer that entered my life. It was a catalyst for profound growth and transformation, reminding me of the importance of opening my heart and embracing the adventure of love. It taught me to cherish each moment, to live authentically, and to extend love and compassion to every aspect of my being.

And so my story continues as a testament to the power of love, resilience, and the unwavering belief that everything happens for a reason. Through my journey, I have discovered the transformative potential that lies within each of us. May my experiences inspire you to embark on your own self-discovery path, open your heart wide, and embrace the adventure of love and healing that awaits you.

The next time you find yourself facing pain or discomfort, I encourage you to pause and embark on a journey of internal reflection. While seeking the quick fix of pharmaceutical drugs from a medical doctor is always an option, why not explore the possibility of healing yourself without the potential side effects? By creating a healthy balance between the pharmaceutical world and tapping into your own innate healing capabilities, you open yourself up to a world of possibilities. Embracing the emotional and spiritual aspects of our health is just as vital as attending to the physical. By delving into the depths of your being, you may uncover the keys to unlocking your own healing potential and finding solace and strength in the most unexpected places.

Start by asking yourself questions about the emotions associated with the area of pain or disease. Allow yourself to release any doubts about uncovering the root cause of these feelings. Honesty and openness with oneself are key in this journey. Then, as you begin to unravel the layers, question how these emotions found their way into your body and why they have taken hold. Finally, accept these feelings for what they are—valuable experiences that have shaped your journey thus far.

Becoming aware of your emotions is a significant step forward. By shining a light on them, you diminish their power and gain the ability to choose how you feel about the underlying issues. Remember that your body is an incredible instrument that can guide you toward emotional, energetic, and spiritual growth. Approach the exploration of your inner landscape with an open mind, personal honesty, and a willingness to reflect deeply. Armed with these tools, you have the power to unearth the root causes of your concerns and leave them behind for good.

What specific emotions do you notice in the area where you feel pain or discomfort?

When I focus on the location of pain, I notice that I feel ________________

Do you have any doubts or resistance about diving deeper into these emotions? If so, what are they?

*I find myself hesitating to explore these emotions because*________________

____

*When I think about delving deeper into these emotions, the doubts and resistance that arise are*____

____

Be completely honest with yourself about the presence of these emotions and their impact on your well-being. What are their effects?

To be completely honest with myself, I understand that these emotions have been affecting ____

____

____

How do you believe these emotions found their way into your body? Are there specific events, experiences, or relationships that come to mind?

I believe these emotions found their way into my body from ______________

____

What underlying beliefs or thought patterns might have contributed to the development or persistence of these emotions?

*The recurring themes in my thoughts and beliefs contributing to these emotions are*____

____

How have these emotions taken hold in your body? Do you notice any physical sensations or patterns associated with them?

*I often notice physical sensations or patterns such as*____________________

____

____

What lessons or insights can you gain from accepting these feelings as valuable experiences? How have they shaped your journey thus far?

Accepting these feelings as valuable experiences teaches me ______________

____

____

What steps can you take to release and heal these emotions? Do any practices, therapies, or self-care strategies resonate with you?

Some practices, therapies, or self-care strategies that resonate with me are

____

____

How can you cultivate compassion and forgiveness towards yourself, and others involved in these emotional experiences?

*I can start by offering myself compassion and forgiveness by*______________

____

____

What vision do you hold for your future well-being? How can you integrate this newfound awareness into your daily life to support your mind-body connection?

*To support my mind-body connection, I can integrate this newfound awareness into my daily life by*____

____

The power of visualization and imagery in the realm of healing is immense. By tapping into the mind-body connection, you can unlock the potential to promote healing and release emotional blockages that may be affecting your well-being. Visualizations provide a bridge between our conscious and subconscious minds, allowing us to access the deeper layers of our being and create positive shifts within ourselves. In this section, we will explore a variety of visualizations and tools that can aid in the process of self-healing. These techniques can be adapted and personalized to suit your unique needs, empowering you to embark on a journey of holistic healing and transformation. Let your imagination soar as you delve into the world of visualization for self-healing and discover the remarkable capabilities of the mind-body connection.

Powerful Imagery Tools for Healing Illness and Disease

SEP - Smart Energy Packs:

- Visualization: Imagine small, Pac-man-like "swarming bees" made of healing energy. See them targeting the area of pain or infection within your body, taking small bites out of it, and removing the negative energy. Visualize these energetic bees working diligently to restore balance and promote healing in that specific area.

Explosion:

- Visualization: Envision a powerful explosion of vibrant light within your body. See this explosion engulfing and dispersing any disease or ailment, completely clearing it from your system. Visualize the healing light transforming and revitalizing every cell, promoting rapid healing, and restoring your body to optimal health.

Lightning Bolt:

- Visualization: Imagine brilliant lightning bolts striking your body with immense power. See these bolts of energy penetrating the affected area, resetting, and recalibrating it. Visualize the electric energy coursing through your body, neutralizing any disease or imbalance and restoring a healthy and harmonious state.

Visualization Techniques for Specific Areas of the Body

Heart Area / Emotional Healing:

- Visualization: Imagine a warm, soothing light enveloping your heart area, melting away any emotional pain or burdens. See this light expanding with each breath, filling your entire being with love and compassion.
- Tools: Practice deep breathing exercises to invite relaxation and release emotional tension. Engage in activities that bring you joy and connect you with positive emotions.

Throat Area / Expression and Communication:

- Visualization: Envision a clear, blue sky stretching above your throat area. Visualize any blockages or suppressed emotions dissolving into the sky, allowing your authentic voice to flow freely.
- Tools: Engage in journaling or expressive writing to explore and express your thoughts and emotions. Engage in conversations that allow you to communicate your needs and feelings effectively.

Solar Plexus Area / Personal Power and Confidence:

- Visualization: Picture a bright, radiant sun shining in your solar plexus area. Feel its warmth and energy, empowering you to release self-doubt and embrace your personal power and confidence.
- Tools: Practice positive affirmations to boost self-esteem and assertiveness. Engage in activities that challenge you and help you step outside your comfort zone.

Abdominal Area / Emotional Release and Creativity:

- Visualization: Imagine a gentle stream of water flowing through your abdomen. With each breath, see this stream washing away stagnant emotions and nurturing your creative energy.
- Tools: Engage in creative outlets such as painting, writing, or dancing to express and release emotions. Practice gentle abdominal exercises or yoga poses to promote emotional and physical well-being.

Lower Back / Grounding and Stability:

- Visualization: Picture the roots of a strong tree growing from the base of your spine deep into the earth. Feel yourself rooted and grounded, releasing any fears or insecurities and gaining a sense of stability.
- Tools: Spend time in nature, practice grounding exercises like walking barefoot on the earth, or engage in grounding meditation practices. Engage in activities that promote a sense of stability and security in your life.

Overall Healing Visualizations

Tree of Healing:

- Visualization: Imagine yourself as a strong, resilient tree firmly rooted in the earth. Visualize healing energy flowing up from the ground, nourishing your roots, and spreading throughout your entire being. See this energy transforming any areas affected by disease or illness, bringing vitality and restoration.

Ocean of Healing Waves:

- Visualization: Picture yourself standing on the shore of a serene ocean. Visualize healing waves gently washing over your body, carrying away any illness or imbalance. Feel the soothing and rejuvenating power of the ocean's healing energy, restoring health and well-being.

Inner Healer:

- Visualization: Close your eyes and visualize a radiant, healing light within you. Imagine this light growing brighter and more expansive, filling every cell of your body. See this light targeting and dissolving any diseased or affected areas, promoting healing, and restoring balance and harmony.

Healing Garden:

- Visualization: Envision yourself in a peaceful, beautiful garden filled with vibrant flowers, lush greenery, and tranquility. Picture yourself walking through the garden, absorbing its healing energy, and allowing it to permeate every part of your body. Visualize the flowers blooming and the garden coming alive as a reflection of your own healing and rejuvenation.

Energy Cleansing:

- Visualization: Imagine standing under a refreshing waterfall or taking a dip in a cleansing river. Visualize the water washing away toxins, disease, or negative energy from your body. Feel the purifying and revitalizing effects of the water, leaving you cleansed, refreshed, and restored.

These visualizations are intended to support and enhance your overall well-being but should not replace professional medical advice or treatment. Use these tools to complement any necessary medical care and consult with healthcare professionals regarding specific health concerns. Visualization can be a powerful tool for promoting a positive mindset and supporting the healing process.

19

Finding Strength in Vulnerability

"Only by embracing vulnerability and imperfections can we fully experience love, connection, and healing."

- John Mark Green

Unlocking the Path to Emotional Healing

Life can throw unexpected challenges our way. Sometimes those challenges come in the form of an accident, a terrible disease, a life-altering sickness, or a death of a loved one. For some of us, it's so easy to bury our emotions, don the superhero cape, and present a powerful, in-control outlook to the world. We worry about showing our pain, fearing that our dearest ones will hurt for us. We convince ourselves that we must be strong for their sake and for our own. But in the midst of this courageous facade, we often forget the importance of giving ourselves permission to grieve. It is okay to care for your own emotional well-being alongside the physical and lifestyle changes you may be making.

I vividly remember the days following my brother's untimely passing. The weight of sorrow settled upon our family, casting a shadow of grief that seemed insurmountable. In the midst of this heartbreaking loss, I found myself grappling with emotions I had never confronted before.

Growing up, our family had a tendency to adopt a "pucker up buttercup" approach when it came to dealing with difficult emotions. We learned to hide our pain, put on a brave face, and navigate through life's challenges without fully acknowledging the depths of our grief. It was a coping mechanism that became ingrained within us, but one that ultimately prevented us from fully processing our emotions and seeking the support we desperately needed.

As I reflect upon those dark days, I realize now that I missed an opportunity to truly mourn my brother's passing and seek solace in my family's embrace. I was so consumed by the fear of burdening others with my suffering that I kept my pain hidden, believing it was my burden to bear alone.

It was not until my battle with cancer that I began to understand the importance of opening up, trusting others with my suffering, and allowing myself to grieve openly. The first days following my cancer diagnosis, overwhelming fear and uncertainty consumed me, and yet again, I felt compelled to keep it all to myself.

I didn't want others to grieve for me, and I thought that by sharing my pain, I would burden them with my struggles. I tried to maintain a sense of normalcy and avoid the "pity party" I believed sharing my diagnosis would bring. I wanted to be seen as a powerful woman who could overcome anything, refusing to succumb to the role of a victim. But deep down, I was scared. I grappled with my emotions, desperately needing an outlet for the whirlwind of thoughts and fears swirling within me.

Facing my own mortality brought me face to face with the fragility of life and the urgency to embrace every emotion that came my way. I consciously decided to stop hiding my suffering and trust others with the depths of my pain. I realized that by keeping my struggles hidden, I was denying myself the opportunity to lean on those who cared about me, share the weight of my burdens, and receive the love and support I desperately needed.

It was a transformative shift, an awakening to the power of vulnerability and the strength that comes from allowing others to hold space for our pain. I discovered that sharing our vulnerabilities allows us to find solace and understanding and create connections that can mend even the deepest wounds.

I was fortunate to have my husband by my side, a pillar of strength and unwavering support. I could share my deepest concerns, fears, and vulnerabilities with him. He listened without judgment, offering words of encouragement and comfort in my darkest moments. Through his presence, I learned the power of vulnerability and the strength it takes to show our true selves. I realized that by opening up and sharing my deepest emotions, I would not be seen as a victim but rather as a courageous warrior navigating her way through a challenging journey.

Looking back, I now understand that finding the balance between sharing our struggles and maintaining our strength is a delicate dance. It's important to honor our emotions and give ourselves permission to grieve, to feel the pain and uncertainty that comes with life-altering challenges. By doing so, we allow others to truly see us, support us, and offer their love and care. It's a profound act of self-compassion to acknowledge our vulnerability and embrace the support surrounding us.

If you find yourself in a situation grappling with the decision to face your deepest emotions or keep them hidden, remember that it's not selfish to be vulnerable and grieve. Give yourself permission to care for your emotional well-being alongside the physical and lifestyle changes you may make. Allow yourself to lean on those who love you to share your fears and concerns. You are not burdening them; you are allowing them the opportunity to be there for you in the most genuine and meaningful way.

Together, let us learn to embrace our pain, trust in the healing process, and honor the memory of my brother by finding solace and growth in the shared journey of grief and healing.

You can navigate the complexities of your journey, finding strength, support, and healing along the way.

Acknowledging Your Emotions: When faced with a life-altering challenge, it's natural to experience a wide range of emotions. These emotions can be overwhelming, from fear and anger to sadness and confusion. Giving yourself the time and space to absorb and feel them is crucial. Allow yourself to sit with these emotions, cry, scream, or simply be still. Embrace the fullness of your feelings without judgment or pressure to be strong. Remember that your emotions are valid, and allowing yourself to experience them opens the door to healing.

Reflect on the emotions you experienced when facing a life-altering diagnosis or challenging situation. How would you describe the range of emotions you experienced?

*When I first received the news, I felt*______________________________

____

*The emotions that overwhelmed me were*___________________________

____

*Allowing myself to feel these emotions fully is important because*__________

____

*In this moment of vulnerability, I can*______________________________

____

Permission to Grieve: Grieving is not limited to the loss of a loved one; it extends to any significant loss or hardship we experience, including our own health challenges. It is essential to give yourself permission to grieve. Allow yourself to mourn the life you had envisioned, the dreams you may have put on hold, and the changes that lie ahead. Give yourself the space to grieve the loss of your physical abilities, the impact on your relationships, and the uncertainty of the future. This grieving process is a testament to your strength and resilience, allowing you to release the weight of expectations and embrace your present reality.

Explore the concept of grieving beyond the loss of a loved one and how it relates to your own challenges. Why is it important to give yourself permission to grieve when facing health challenges or significant losses?

*Giving myself permission to grieve means*______________________________

____

What aspects of your life or future did you need to mourn or let go of?

*I found myself needing to mourn and let go of*__________________________

____

In what ways can you grant yourself the space and time to grieve those losses?

*In order to honor my emotions and process my losses, I will*_______________

____

How has embracing the grieving process allowed you to find strength and acceptance in your present reality?

*By fully embracing the grieving process, I have been able to find strength and acceptance in my present reality as I*_____________________________

____

Seeking Support: You don't have to navigate this journey alone. Seeking support from loved ones, friends, or professionals can provide the solace and understanding you need. Share your feelings openly and honestly and allow others to be there for you. Their presence and support can offer a sense of comfort and remind you that you are not alone. Connecting with support groups or seeking the guidance of a therapist can also provide a safe space to process your emotions and gain valuable insights from others who have walked a similar path.

Who can you contact for support during a challenging time, and why?

*During a challenging time, I can reach out to*______________________
*for support because*____

____

____

How can the support of loved ones, friends, or professionals help you navigate your journey?

*Having support can make a significant difference in my journey by*_______

____

____

Have you explored support groups or therapy? If so, what insights or benefits have you gained from these experiences?

I have explored _________________ *and have gained insights and benefits such as*____

____

Embracing Healing: As you give yourself permission to grieve, remember that healing is not about erasing the pain or denying its existence. Healing is a gradual process that involves finding inner peace and cultivating resilience. Allow yourself to acknowledge the pain and embrace the moments of joy and gratitude that may arise along the way. Focus on self-care, nourishing your body, mind, and spirit. Engage in activities that bring you comfort and solace. Practice mindfulness and meditation to cultivate a sense of inner calm and resilience. By embracing healing, you create space for growth, transformation, and the emergence of a renewed sense of self.

What practices or activities do you engage in to support your healing journey?

Supporting my healing journey involves engaging in practices or activities like

____

____

How do you acknowledge the pain and challenges while embracing moments of joy and gratitude?

*Finding the balance between acknowledging the pain and embracing joy and gratitude involves*____

____

How does practicing self-care, mindfulness, or meditation contribute to your sense of inner calm and resilience?

*Practicing self-care, mindfulness, or meditation contributes to my sense of inner calm and resilience by*____

____

Giving yourself permission to grieve is a courageous act of self-love and acceptance. It's about acknowledging your emotions, honoring your journey, and seeking support when needed. For some of us, it can be challenging to let go of the superhero cape and allow ourselves to grieve openly. But by doing so, we create an opportunity for authentic healing and transformation. My friend, please embrace the necessary step of grieving alongside the physical and lifestyle changes you are making. Remember that you are not defined by your illness or diagnosis. Your strength and resilience lie within, waiting to be unleashed. Give yourself permission and embrace the transformative power of self-compassion and healing.

20

Embracing the Divine in Relationships

"Relationships are like a dance. Sometimes they flow effortlessly, and other times they require patience, forgiveness, and a willingness to step back and let the other lead."

-Unknown

From Me to We

It's often said that there's no such thing as a perfect relationship. But hold on a second! Isn't everyone a perfectly divine, if slightly confused, piece of the cosmic puzzle? Navigating relationships is like trying to assemble a puzzle without the picture on the box. But fear not! With some conscious effort, we can transform the process into something akin to a well-choreographed dance or a carefully crafted symphony.

You see, relationships are as diverse as the array of characters in a bustling city. Each type, each dynamic, and each interaction provides a platform for growth, strength, and independence. The most harmonious relationships are those built on a foundation of truth, much like a sturdy treehouse. You know, the one that doesn't collapse when the wind of life gets a little gusty. It's a place where hidden secrets, covert agendas, and rampaging egos are left at the door. These relationships communicate like seasoned diplomats, support each other like the best spotter at a gymnastics meet, and weather storms without turning into a soap opera.

In the grand buffet of relationships, we all have the sweet and sour, sometimes spicy, soulmate relationships. These soulmates often mirror our most significant differences, pushing our buttons and triggering emotional fireworks. Often, these soulmates are found in our parents, siblings, and children—the same ones who likely stole your candy as a kid. They offer a roller coaster ride of learning and growth, testing our patience, stirring our stress, and giving us countless opportunities for love, forgiveness, release, and healing.

Then, we have the drama maestros, those who could win an Oscar for their performance in the victim role. They seem to relish in amplifying minor issues until they resemble Godzilla-sized problems. Instead of reflecting on their part, they prefer to point fingers, raise their voices, ghost you, or even aim for your soul with their words. These kinds of relationships could give a rollercoaster a run for its money in terms of emotional ups and downs.

Navigating relationships is like walking a tightrope while juggling flaming torches—it's complex and sometimes risky, but each step forward is a catalyst for growth. It prompts us to explore the depth of our emotional resilience and ability for love while teaching us that sometimes the best thing to do is laugh at the absurdity of it all.

Navigating the Quicksand's of Unhealthy Relationships

In the grand adventure that is life, we all form a fascinating tapestry of beliefs and patterns about love and relationships. These are informed by our parents, friends, the community, the media, and our own individual experiences—the whole gamut from rosy rom-coms to tear-jerking tragedies. Some of these beliefs are like cozy blankets, wrapping us up in warmth, acceptance, and unconditional love. Others, however, are like ill-fitting shoes, squeezing us into shapes and behavior patterns that do not honor our authentic selves. Let's shine a light on some of these murky misinterpretations of love that can lead us into the quicksand's of toxic relationships:

1. **The Bedroom Barter**: "If I have sex, then I will be loved." Let's clear this up right away. Love and sex can be as different as apples and oranges. When we're craving love and affection, sex can be like a fast-food meal—briefly satisfying but lacking in long-term nourishment. Genuine love is a rich, multi-course feast that deeply fulfills you.
2. **The Material Mirage**: "Money and gifts make me feel loved." Money and valuables may provide a fleeting sense of security, but they can't buy love. While gifts can spark temporary joy, remember that love isn't up for auction. It can't be bought or sold. Love is the priceless gift that keeps on giving.
3. **The Illness Illusion**: "I must be sick to be loved." Some people learned early on that playing the patient earned them attention. Yet this is not genuine care; it's a performance aimed at manipulation. In a healthy relationship, love is freely given, not extracted through manufactured crises.
4. **The Suffering Syndrome**: "I have to suffer to get love." Those who've endured pain or abuse may confuse love with suffering. Love isn't a thorny rosebush that draws blood; it's a gentle breeze that soothes and uplifts.
5. **The Fixer Fallacy**: "I must fix others to be loved." The urge to play the hero can stem from an underlying sense of worthlessness. Love isn't a damsel in distress needing to be rescued; it's a partner standing shoulder-to-shoulder with you.
6. **The Control Conundrum**: "I have to be in control." For some, having control offers a sense of safety and prevents them from feeling victimized again. It's like they're saying, "I'll control you before you control me." But true love isn't a game of chess to be controlled. It's a dance that requires flexibility, compromise, and trust.

7. **The People-Pleaser Pitfall**: "I must please others to be loved." Constantly striving for approval can be exhausting. People pleasers crave approval, and they equate it with love. They may try to be perfect for you until they burn out, much like an overeager puppy constantly seeking a pat on the head. Remember that love isn't a demanding taskmaster. It's an accepting friend that appreciates you for who you are.
8. **The Abandonment Anxiety**: "If I love you, you will leave me." Fear of abandonment can lead to self-sabotaging relationships. Some folks have been hurt by loss, betrayal, or abandonment, so they sabotage relationships before they can progress. It's like planting a rose bush only to mow it down before it can bloom. Love isn't a ticking time bomb set to explode; it's a safe space to grow and evolve together.
9. **The Hurt Hypothesis**: "Love hurts." This belief can trap us in painful, unhealthy relationships. Real love doesn't hurt. It heals, nurtures, and supports.

As we've journeyed through the myriad hues of relationships—from the sweet and sour soulmate bonds to the rollercoaster dynamics with drama maestros—it's clear that our interpersonal connections are intricate tapestries woven with threads of emotion, experience, and belief. Each relationship, with its unique patterns and lessons, forms a chapter in our ever-evolving story of growth and understanding. Now, I'd like you to take a moment and think about your own experiences. We're going to dive a little deeper, reflect on the roles you've taken on, and the beliefs you might have unconsciously adopted. Ready for some thought-provoking questions? Let's peel back the layers and really explore what makes your relationships tick.

What does a "sturdy treehouse" relationship look like to you?

*For me, a relationship built on a solid foundation means*_______________

____

Who are the "spicy" soulmate relationships that push your buttons in your life?

*I've noticed the people who push my buttons the most are*_______________

____

How have media portrayals of love and relationships influenced your understanding of them?

*Growing up, I was influenced by movies and shows that suggested*________

____

How do you differentiate between genuine love, infatuation, or other fleeting emotions?

*To me, genuine love feels different from infatuation because*_____________

____

Which of the mentioned unhealthy relationship beliefs resonates most with you and why?

*The belief that really struck a chord with me is*______________________

*Because*_______________________________________

What beliefs or patterns about love were you raised with? Do you still hold onto them?

*Growing up, I was taught that love meant*_________________________

____

Navigating relationships is an intricate dance—one that requires introspection, understanding, and, above all, self-awareness. As we've explored together today, every relationship holds a mirror to our inner world, reflecting both our strengths and areas for growth. Remember that understanding these intricate dynamics and our role within them truly unlocks the power to build fulfilling, meaningful connections. I encourage you to reflect on these questions regularly, cherish the lessons you uncover, and let them guide you on your journey to deeper, more authentic relationships. Embrace the dance, cherish the symphony, and most importantly, trust in the journey.

21

Building Healthy Boundaries

"Embracing self-love means bravely drawing lines that honor our values and preserve our emotional balance."

- Unknown

Guardrails of Life

As a child, I was the ideal people pleaser, always trying to fit into the mold others had crafted for me, even when it seemed like they were rooting for my downfall. Picture a stand-up comic trying to win over a crowd that's just waiting for the next pie-in-the-face gag. Let me give you an example. When I was a little three-year-old lass, a neighborhood bully tried to convince me that his dog's poop was a delectable chocolate treat. You could say his persuasive skills were, well, crappy.

Despite the "need to please" deeply ingrained in me, I knew there was no way I was going to eat it. So I pulled a magic trick of my own—a sleight of hand, if you will—and pretended to lick the poop, grimaced, and spat. The neighborhood jury erupted in laughter, and I walked home, my face a crimson canvas of embarrassment.

Many years and many so-called friends later, I decided it was high time to step out of the shadow of people-pleasing. I stood my ground, found my voice, and said, "No more." Yet, in my quest for self-assertion, I teetered dangerously close to the other extreme, giving off a vibe that screamed, "It's my way or the highway."

Navigating the treacherous seas of boundary-setting was, and still is, a lifelong journey. I've learned to respect my limits and protect myself from being hurt again. But I've also found it challenging to strike a balance that does not alienate my loved ones while preserving my sense of self.

Living in Hawaii, I often play host to a variety of guests, offering a constant stream of opportunities to refine my boundary-setting skills. Most guests are lovely, but then there are those who seem to have attended the 'How to Be a Challenging Guest 101' course.

One such encounter involved a distant acquaintance and her stepdaughter. As I opened the doors of my home, I shared with them the story of my journey towards holistic living, shaped by my personal experience of overcoming breast cancer. With honesty and vulnerability, I expressed my ongoing recovery from recent hand surgery and the occasional need for a helping hand. Their response was filled with enthusiasm and willingness to lend a helping hand, creating a sense of shared understanding and support during their stay.

The ideal scenario would have been for my guests to contribute by cleaning up after themselves, helping with meals and dishes, and generally being respectful. But as is often the case in the school of life, things didn't quite go as planned.

By day three, I was exhausted from playing the roles of a house cleaner, chef, and all-around servant. I asked for a bit of help, only to be met with resentment and a refusal to contribute. It was a harsh reminder that not everyone shares the same common sense or definition of etiquette.

The tension escalated until it culminated in a painful confrontation. My friend lashed out, and I was left feeling used, abused, and belittled in my own home. It was as if a dark cloud of negativity had taken up residence in my house.

In the end, they packed their bags and left, leaving me with a valuable lesson. It was a wake-up call about the importance of setting clear boundaries from the get-go, even if it's uncomfortable.

I've come to understand that my heart deserves to be served first. Only then can I genuinely serve others in a way that aligns with my highest self. To my friend, wherever you are now, I hope you find healing for the pain you carry. I'm grateful for the lessons I learned through our interaction, and I wish you well on your journey.

A POISON TREE

I was angry with my friend;
I told my wrath, my wrath did end.
I was angry with my foe,
I told it not, my wrath did grow.
And I watered it in fears,
Night and morning with my tears;
And I sunned it with smiles,
And with soft deceitful wiles.
And it grew both day and night,
Till it bore an apple bright;
And my foe beheld it shine,
And he knew that it was mine,
And into my garden stole
When the night had veiled the pole;
In the morning glad I see
My foe outstretched beneath the tree.

William Blake (1757-1827)

Having shared my personal experience of overcoming people-pleasing tendencies and establishing boundaries in relationships, I hope you can relate to the struggles and growth involved in such a journey. Just as one would wrestle with the poisonous tree of folklore, wrestling its venomous branches and navigating its treacherous roots, each one of us has to face the challenges of our own personal 'poison trees' in the form of toxic relationships.

In sharing my journey, I hope to offer some insight into the struggles and victories that come with navigating these metaphorical poison trees. We each have our unique story and set of experiences. Therefore, taking a step back and reflecting on your relationships, beliefs, and behaviors is crucial.

This introspection can be challenging, yet it's a vital step toward recognizing and breaking free from the toxic patterns that entangle us. Just as one would learn to avoid the poisonous fruit of the tree, we must learn to recognize and avoid the toxic behaviors that harm us.

Remember that honesty with yourself is the key to unlocking genuine growth and healing. It's the antidote to the poison, the sunshine that allows a healthier tree to grow in place of the old, toxic one. It's your journey, your adventure. Be brave and take the first step, for your vibrant garden awaits.

What beliefs and behaviors do you exhibit to maintain a relationship?

*In my relationships, I tend to*______________________________

____

Are there any conditions in your current or past relationships?

In my relationships, I have experienced situations such as ____________

____

Do you feel obligated to do something or be a certain way to stay in a relationship?

To stay in a relationship, I have felt obligated to ________________

____

____

What do you consider a toxic relationship?

A toxic relationship, in my opinion, is ______________________________

____

What toxic relationships do you currently have or have had in the past?

The toxic relationships I have experienced include ____________________

____

____

How have these toxic relationships affected you and your life?

These toxic relationships have affected my life by ____________________

____

____

What positive steps can you take to prevent these relationships from continuing to affect you negatively?

To minimize the negative impact of toxic relationships, I can ____________

____

____

How will taking these steps benefit your relationships?

By taking these steps, my relationships will __________________________

____

____

By implementing these changes, what do you envision your relationships looking like six months from now?

*In six months, I expect my relationships to be*__________________________

____

____

____

Imagine you're an intrepid explorer navigating the treacherous terrain of toxic relationships. Invisible chains shackle you, a marionette entangled in a twisted drama. Remember this—you are no Pinocchio, no puppet to be manipulated. You are a courageous adventurer; the only character you can truly control is yourself.

In this epic journey called life, if you find yourself feeling like a well-worn treasure map, repeatedly trampled underfoot, remember that you are not auditioning for the role of a doormat. You are the hero of this quest and deserve a hero's celebration, not to be stepped on. It's time to sever the puppet strings of these relationships and declare your independence. Take a moment to cheer for yourself for having the audacity to cry out, "Enough!"

This quest isn't just about escaping the venomous branches of the poison tree. It's also about cultivating a lush, vibrant garden within your heart, where love, respect, and self-worth can blossom. As you embark on this journey, you'll encounter challenges and trials, but you'll also discover hidden treasures within yourself—strengths and abilities you never knew you possessed. With each step, you'll shed the weight of the toxic past, making room for healthier relationships and a brighter future.

Unleash yourself; let the winds of change carry away your anger. You're on a quest to find your true self, be a beacon of resilience, and dance to the rhythm of your own heartbeat. Your life is your adventure, and you're the hero. Make it a quest worth remembering.

The Art of Boundary Setting

Embrace the opportunity to learn from past relationships and create the boundaries necessary to prevent another relationship disaster. But first, let's clarify that boundaries are not about building walls, pushing people away, cutting them off without allowing a response, or giving someone the silent treatment. These actions are forms of emotional abuse, not boundaries.

Boundaries are the limits we set for ourselves within our relationships with others. They prevent unhealthy dynamics, like feeling taken advantage of when a friend repeatedly asks you for money. Boundaries help us determine our comfort zones and how we wish to be treated.

Establishing boundaries in all areas of life where we interact with others, including family, friends, romance, work, and social media relationships, is crucial. By doing so, we discern which relationships are healthy and which are not. Boundaries come in various forms, such as physical, sexual, emotional, mental, spiritual, religious, financial, material, time, personal space, home, and work.

Permit yourself to set boundaries, express your needs, and liberate yourself from toxic relationships that breed resentment, manipulation, and abuse. Setting boundaries is neither bad nor selfish. It's normal to feel discomfort when you're unaccustomed to asserting your desires with certain people or in specific situations. There's no need to feel guilty, anxious, or obligated to over-explain yourself or apologize for establishing boundaries. Everyone has the right to communicate their preferences. If someone challenges you by ignoring or pushing against your boundaries, the relationship is likely already unhealthy and may need to end.

Establishing and keeping boundaries with friends requires mutual trust and respect. It's equally important to respect others' boundaries, whether they're parents, children, romantic partners, managers, coworkers, or anyone else we interact with. Understanding and honoring each other's boundaries is an invaluable tool for fostering balanced and harmonious relationships.

How would you define personal boundaries?

Personal boundaries, in my understanding, are ______________________

____

Reflect on a time when someone crossed your boundaries. How did it make you feel, and what did you do about it?

There was a time when someone overstepped my boundaries ____________

____

____

Think about your current relationships. Are there any boundaries you feel you need to establish or strengthen?

*Looking at my current relationships, I feel I need to establish or strengthen the following boundaries*______________________________

____

In what ways do you communicate your boundaries to others?

*When it comes to communicating my boundaries to others, I usually*______

____

____

How do you react when someone doesn't respect your boundaries?

*When someone does not respect my boundaries, I typically react by*________

____

____

How do you respect the boundaries of others in your life?

*Respecting the boundaries of others in my life involves*________________

____

____

What challenges have you faced when trying to establish boundaries?

*In my experience, the challenges I've faced when establishing boundaries include*____________________________________

____

____

What positive changes have you noticed in your life and relationships since establishing more precise boundaries?

Since establishing more precise boundaries, I've noticed positive changes, such as

____

____

Can you identify any patterns in the boundaries you often feel are crossed (e.g., emotional, physical, time)?

*Reflecting on situations where my boundaries were crossed, I can identify patterns related to*____________________________

____

____

How do you plan to keep and uphold your boundaries in the future?

*To keep and uphold my boundaries in the future, I plan to*_____________

____

____

Setting boundaries isn't just about drawing a line in the sand; it's about asserting your worth and protecting your peace. Boundaries are akin to mapping out your personal territory in the vast landscape of human interactions. By clearly defining what you're comfortable with, you're protecting your peace and well-being and fostering a sense of mutual respect with those around you. Remember, boundaries aren't about shutting people out but inviting them into a space where both parties can thrive. It's a declaration of self-worth, a testament to your self-awareness, and a commitment to nurturing healthy, balanced relationships. As you journey forward, may your boundaries serve as beacons, guiding you toward genuine connections and honoring the beautiful, unique individual that you are.

22

Nurturing Open and Honest Communication

When we embrace vulnerability and share our truths, we invite others to do the same, nurturing a space of openness and empathy."

- Unknown

Unlocking Authentic Connections

In the intricate web of relationships, open and honest communication stands as the golden thread binding hearts together, while respecting boundaries forms the delicate tapestry that prevents the unraveling of our lives.

Before we delve into the art of open and honest communication, let's emphasize the critical importance of emotional self-regulation. Keeping silent, stewing in anger, and replaying the drama in your head does nothing but bring misery to everyone involved. Like a ship needs a skilled captain to navigate stormy seas, emotional regulation allows us to steer through turbulent emotions before communicating. The sea of emotions needs to be calmed before meaningful dialogue can begin.

Silence and simmering anger, when left unchecked, sow seeds of misery. Bottling up emotions and letting anger simmer is as helpful as shaking a soda can and hoping it won't explode when you open it. These unresolved feelings accumulate like molten lava within a volcano, just waiting for that perfect moment to erupt and rain hot, molten discomfort all over your relationships. This eruption can cause untold damage to the connections you hold dear. To avoid this volcanic emotional mess, we need a plan.

Picture this—you're about to send a fiery text message to your friend, but before you hit send, you realize it might not be the best idea. Instead, you put your phone down, take a deep breath, and go for a walk. This act of stepping back and giving yourself time to cool down is like finding a fire extinguisher just in time — it prevents the blaze from spreading.

Another example could be when you feel a surge of frustration during a conversation with your partner. Instead of escalating the argument, you decide to pause the discussion, go to a quiet space, and engage in deep breathing exercises. This momentary pause helps you regain emotional balance, so when you return to the conversation, it's from a calmer and more rational standpoint.

Now, you might be wondering, how long should I let the emotional volcano simmer down? Well, it's like brewing a pot of tea—it depends on the blend. Some emotions may need a brief steeping, while others might require a longer infusion. The key is to have a predetermined self-imposed time limit to regain composure before engaging in communication.

Taking a step back and allowing yourself time to breathe, reflect, and process your emotions can help you approach the situation with a more balanced, rational mindset. This cooling-off period enables you to release the pressure that has built up within, minimizing the risk of an emotional explosion. By processing your emotions and gaining a fresh perspective, you can return to the situation with greater understanding, empathy, and effective communication. In doing so, you'll be promoting healthier, more open relationships and a more balanced emotional life.

When the volcano of emotions threatens to erupt, how will you personally simmer down and regain composure before engaging in communication? For instance, do you have specific strategies or techniques that you find effective in diffusing emotional tension?

To simmer down and regain composure before engaging in communication, I can implement some effective strategies, such as ______________________

____

Giving Voice to Feelings

No matter how absurd or far-fetched you believe your feelings may seem, there's merit in expressing them. You see, your words are your key to freedom, and your loved ones—they are the gatekeepers. So summon your courage, detach, simmer down, and communicate your true feelings. You might find that what was once an uncomfortable confrontation morphs into a beautiful heart-to-heart, culminating in a hug that heals.

Have you ever savored the silence after a thunderstorm? That precious pause, filled with relief and a promise of renewal? That's the power of letting your feelings flow, clearing the air, and allowing sunshine to follow the storm. Let's not fool ourselves into believing that our hearts can serve as bottomless vessels for pent-up emotions. You deserve to express your feelings, no matter how absurd they may seem to others. And they deserve to listen, to really hear what's bubbling beneath your calm exterior.

Now, take a moment to reflect on the relationships you want to nurture and bring to new heights. Who are the individuals in your love, family, friend, and work relationships that deserve to engage in honest conversations with you? Make a list of these significant connections.

Love Relationships: ________________________________

____

Family Relationships: ______________________________

____

Friend Relationships: ____

____

Work Relationships: ____

____

Choose at least one individual you have hushed up and barricaded off who deserves an opportunity for healing through sincere communication. Who can you commit to have a full-hearted dialogue with? Who deserves healing through honest communication now?

*The relationship I have stifled or closed off, and whom I am committed to reconnect with is*____

____

Before embarking on the path of reconnection and delving into that crucial conversation, it's essential to equip yourself with a few more keys to unlock the door to authentic and meaningful communication. These keys will not only help you navigate the often-complex terrain of human interaction but also ensure that your dialogue is constructive, empathetic, and conducive to building or mending relationships. Let's explore these vital aspects that can pave the way for a more fruitful exchange of thoughts, feelings, and ideas.

- **Listen Up**

In this journey to heal and strengthen relationships, it's crucial to grasp that listening holds just as much importance as expressing your own feelings. While sharing your thoughts and emotions is vital for open communication, giving others the chance to express their feelings, thoughts, and experiences is equally significant.

Genuine dialogue is a two-way street where understanding flourishes not only through speaking but also through attentive listening. It's in these moments of active listening, where you genuinely focus on what the other person is saying without planning your response in advance. This level of listening nurtures empathy and creates a safe space for authentic conversations, ensuring that both speaking and listening play harmonious roles in the dance of communication while avoiding unnecessary conflicts.

- **Unlock Empathy**

Respecting the feelings and emotions that others express is akin to honoring their unique journey through life. Each person carries within them a rich tapestry of experiences, beliefs, and perspectives that shape the way they perceive the world. Consider a scenario where a close friend comes to you because you have inadvertently offended or hurt them in some way. They've mustered the courage to have an open and honest conversation about their feelings.

In this moment, your friend is unlocking a door to their inner world. They are sharing their vulnerability and discomfort, hoping for understanding and resolution. As they express their thoughts and emotions, they are essentially handing you the key to their emotional well-being. Respecting their words means truly listening, empathizing with their hurt, and taking responsibility for your actions. It's as if you're holding the key to mending the trust and friendship, and by responding with empathy and a sincere apology, you're helping them unlock the door to healing and reconciliation.

This act of sharing is a powerful way to seek connection, understanding, and validation. Your friend is saying, "I see you. I hear you. My feelings matter." In turn, by respecting their words and emotions, you demonstrate that you value their right to express themselves authentically, and you commit to fostering a deeper, more empathetic relationship. Just as you cherish the freedom to voice your thoughts and emotions, so should you honor and protect this right in others. It's a mutual exchange of empathy and understanding that strengthens the bonds of friendship and human connection.

- **Navigate Disagreements with Grace**

In the tapestry of our interactions, disagreements are like colorful threads that can either weave a harmonious pattern or create a tangled mess. Let's imagine these disagreements as the occasional knots in our shoelaces. Instead of letting them escalate into a frustrating tug-of-war, consider the transformative power of a simple phrase: "I haven't thought of that perspective," or "I hear where you're coming from," or even, "You might be right about that." It's like using a bit of friendly shoelace magic to ease those knots, turning a potentially knotty situation into a meaningful exchange of ideas and emotions.

It's essential to remember that when you say, "You might be right about that," it doesn't necessarily mean you wholeheartedly agree with the other person's viewpoint. Instead, it signifies your willingness to consider their perspective and engage in a more open and constructive conversation. It's a way to acknowledge that there may be validity in what they're saying, even if you ultimately hold a different opinion. This delicate balance allows for respectful disagreement, where two individuals can explore their differences while preserving the dignity and respect essential for healthy relationships. In doing so, we not only foster understanding but also create an atmosphere where diverse opinions can coexist, and where the richness of varied perspectives can contribute to collective growth and wisdom.

In the journey of rekindling connections and opening doors to fresh possibilities, allow your spirit to be the compass guiding your words. Take that first step by initiating a conversation or composing a heartfelt letter to that person who is ready to engage in renewed communication and explore new horizons.

The key to beginning this transformative process is crafting an opener that gently breaks the ice, paving the way for genuine and honest communication. Consider these questions as your guiding stars on this journey:

1. Would you be open to a conversation with me?
2. Our relationship is important to me because … (I've noticed some distance, pain, fear, or walls in our relationship lately.)
3. What have you been experiencing in our relationship?
4. The ways I may have contributed to our situation are … (judging, blaming, resenting, fear, protecting myself, pulling away, etc.)
5. Would you be open to a fresh start or new possibilities in our relationship?
6. From this point forward, you can count on me to …

Picture this communication unfolding. What is your opener to break the ice?

I will open space for the conversation by ______________________________

____

How does the conversation look with judgments and defenses out of the picture?

I envision the conversation ____

____

____

Lastly, lock in time to have this heart-to-heart conversation.

I'll initiate this conversation on ___________________________________

Remember that you're not just a passenger on this voyage; you are the captain of your ship, the author of your story. As you navigate the tumultuous seas of communication, do so with courage, honesty, and compassion.

Relationship Exploration

Now, let's embark on a journey of introspection. Picture a healthy relationship that resonates with your spirit and nurtures your soul. What does such a relationship look like to you?

*In my vision, a healthy relationship is characterized by*________________

____

Which relationships in your life would you classify as healthy and vibrant?

*The relationships in my life that embody health and positivity are*_________

____

Dive deeper into these relationships. How does it feel to be part of such an enriching bond?

*Being in these healthy relationships feels like*___________________________

____

Examine these relationships' impact on your daily life, mood, and overall well-being.

*These healthy relationships influence my life by*__________________________

____

Now, let's identify the secret ingredients that make these relationships flourish. Is it effective listening and communication, unwavering trust, shared laughter, or something else entirely?

*The key elements that make these relationships work so well are*__________

____

Let's rewind to a moment in time when you felt things could have been different in a relationship or social setting. Close your eyes and visualize the scene as vividly as you can. Who are the key players? What emotions are in the air? What are the spoken and unspoken dialogues?

*In that particular moment, the scenario unfolded like*________________

____

____

In this scene, how did you present yourself? What was your demeanor, and how did you react to the circumstances?

*In this situation, my demeanor and reactions were*__________________

____

Reflect on the conversations you had. How did you interact with others and respond to their words or actions?

*In those conversations, I interacted and responded by*________________

____

Now, engage in some introspection. How did your actions or words contribute to the discord that makes you wish things had turned out differently?

*Reflecting on my own actions and words, I realize that*________________

____

____

Armed with hindsight and self-reflection, reimagine the scene. How would it play out in your ideal world? What would change?

If I could rewrite that scene, it would ________________________

____

____

What did you do differently in this revised version of the event?

*In this revised scenario, I acted differently by*____________________

____

____

Taking these insights forward, how will you approach similar situations differently in the future? How will you show up as a more self-aware, considerate version of yourself?

*In future situations, I will show up differently by*_________________

____

____

The journey of authentic communication is a transformative one. It's a path illuminated by empathy, understanding, forgiveness, and a deep respect for the words and emotions of others. As you step into this journey, remember that it's not just about the words you say but the genuine connection you forge. It's about honoring the unique tapestry of experiences that each person carries, and about fostering trust, deepening relationships, and creating a world where diverse viewpoints can coexist harmoniously.

However, it's important to acknowledge that not everyone you encounter may be ready for this level of communication, or for some reason, it might be impossible to engage in a heartfelt conversation with them at this time. In such instances, I offer you "The Journey to Relationship Healing: A Heart-to-Heart Process," a valuable tool for your personal growth and exploration. This process allows you to continue nurturing your own capacity for empathy, understanding, forgiveness, and patience, even when immediate conversations are not possible.

As you embark on this journey of authentic communication, may your words become a bridge, your actions a testament to empathy, and your relationships a source of profound growth and fulfillment, whether through heartfelt conversations or through the transformative power of your own personal growth.

A Journey to Relationship Healing: A Heart-to-Heart Process

Prepare to embark on a healing journey with someone in your life who deserves it. This person could be a friend, a loved one, a child, a parent, a relative, a colleague, or even someone you've yet to meet. You may also choose someone who has passed away or is currently unable to communicate with whom you wish to complete or continue a relationship.

Begin by closing your eyes and placing your hand over your heart. Take a moment to connect with your own heart space, observing its openness to both give and receive love. Imagine your heart as a rose. Is it a tightly wound bud, a fully bloomed flower, or somewhere in between?

Visualize a dazzling, crystal-clear white light above you. As you take nine deep, heartfelt breaths, invite this light to flow into your heart space, nourishing your rose. See the light gently coaxing each petal to unfurl, transforming your rose into a vibrant, open bloom that radiates love and innocence.

When you feel ready, picture the person you've chosen for this healing journey sitting before you. Allow any past conflicts to dissolve, removing any barriers that might exist between you. Look beyond their physical form and see their heart as a rose. What state is it in? Is it a reluctant bud or in full bloom, radiating love?

Now, perceive the clear, bright white light encompassing you both. Feel it flowing down, illuminating both your hearts, and nourishing your roses. As the light fills your roses, imagine it radiating from your heart, creating a bridge of light to theirs.

You've now formed a luminous triangle of light and love, connecting you and the other person. Within this sacred space, open up to a deep, soulful communication. Ask questions, listen to their perspective, and respect the unique journey that has shaped them into who they are today. Share your thoughts and feelings, keeping an open mind and heart to their responses. This communication is not about winning or losing, being right or wrong. It's about understanding and accepting that you are both navigating life as best you can, given your individual experiences and lessons.

Finally, bring your attention back to their rose. Is it opening to your love or closing off? If it doesn't seem to be changing, don't worry. Some roses take more time to open than others. But trust that your love is reaching them on some level; in time, their heart will respond. Remember that this is a journey of patience, love, and understanding. Keep the faith and keep the love flowing.

Restating a fundamental truth is essential—you cannot force anyone to change. Their path to growth and transformation is deeply personal, just like yours. However, don't let this discourage you. The heart-to-heart process we've delved into is powerful, operating not just on a conscious level but seeping into the unconscious realms as well.

By consistently practicing this process, by continuing to send love and light, you are encouraging a safe space for transformation. You are fostering an environment of understanding and mutual growth. And in this space, you might find the person you're in a relationship with starting to open up more. You'll witness walls coming down, conversations flowing more freely, and hearts opening up to possibilities hitherto unseen.

It's the subtle shifts that often make the most significant difference. So keep your heart open, your spirit brave, and your mind receptive to change. Watch as your relationships evolve, grow, and bloom just like the rose in your heart space. As you close this chapter, carry these insights with you and watch the transformative power they can have on your relationships and, by extension, on your life.

Keep on this journey, continue the excellent work you're doing, and be amazed at the unfolding of deeper, more meaningful connections in your life.

23

Unveiling Your True Relationship with Food

"You are what you eat, so don't be fast, cheap, easy, or fake."

-Unknown

A Journey of Nourishment and Self-Love

Do you perceive food as a formidable foe or an agent of change that influences your weight? Has food morphed into a tool of comfort for you, especially during times of stress, sadness, overwhelm, or anxiety? Time to engage in a heartfelt chat with yourself. Grab your pen and write down your current relationship with food, don't shy away from the naked truth.

When I reflect on my current relationship with food, I realize that _______

____

____

____

Consider this: Does your food love you back? I challenge you to view food through the lens of friendship. Is food your dependable buddy, ready to lend an ear (or a bite) during challenging times? Or is your food pal a sweet-talking con artist camouflaged in tantalizing flavors, only to wreak havoc on your hormones and emotions? This unwholesome amigo can put on a tantalizing disguise, but in reality, it hijacks your taste buds and slowly chips away at your well-being.

Imagine ingesting this unhealthy food, masquerading as your friend. Once inside, it becomes the houseguest from hell, refusing to leave and leaving your body in chaos. Like the worst kind of freeloader, it saps your vitality, making you feel lethargic, stressed, and worn out. It will leave you feeling down in the dumps, quite literally. You'll find yourself engaged in a tiring battle, trying to evict this unwanted guest from your body, only to breathe a sigh of relief once it's finally out.

Does it make sense to keep a relationship with something that leaves you feeling ill, guilty, and depressed? The answer is a resounding no. It's time to bid farewell to these unhealthy associations. Purge your pantry of any food that doesn't serve your well-being. You deserve to feel great and consume food supporting your wellness journey.

Take a moment to list all the foods that don't reciprocate your love.

The foods that do not love me back are ______________________________

____

Take a trash bag and bid farewell to these fair-weather food friends. They've been taking you for a ride, and it's time they took a one-way trip to the bin. They're just junk, and that's where they belong.

You'll likely bump into these old 'pals' at the grocery store or a party. You might be tempted to rekindle the friendship, inviting them back into your life (and mouth) at the first opportunity. But HOLD UP! Recall how they treated you, how they toyed with your emotions and saddled you with unwanted weight. Remember the discomfort and distress they caused.

Prepare yourself with backup plans for when you see these old food "friends." Carry new, healthy food options, letting those unwelcome treats know you've moved on to better companions. Write down your emotions and feelings when you crave your old food pals or find something else to focus on.

What will you do when you crave and want to let harmful foods back into your life?

When the craving for harmful foods resurfaces, my plan of action will be

____

____

____

Savoring Life: The Art of Mindful Eating

Embracing mindful eating can elevate an ordinary meal into a spiritual journey, fostering gratitude for the effort behind its creation and unveiling the interconnectedness between our nourishment, well-being, and the health of our planet.

Eating, a simple yet essential act, has sadly morphed into a hurried, mindless routine for many. It's squeezed between meetings, gulped down in front of screens, or even forgotten altogether in the rush of the day. But let's take a step back and remember; food is the life-sustaining fuel that keeps our engines running. Without it, our vitality would quickly deplete. This highlights why it's so crucial to not just eat, but eat well, to truly enrich our lives. How we view food, and our eating practices can be a game-changer for our health and well-being.

Let's explore the concept of mindful eating. This isn't about merely masticating and swallowing; it's about immersing yourself in the entire eating experience. So first things first, turn off those distractions. Whether it's your laptop, TV, or a torrent of thoughts, switch them off. Eating deserves your full attention.

Now, engage all your senses in this culinary journey. Marvel at the colors and shapes on your plate, let the tantalizing aroma waft into your nostrils, and let each flavor sing on your tongue. Chew slowly, savoring the symphony of textures in your mouth. Eating isn't a sprint; it's a marathon. Taking even five to ten minutes to truly relish your food can make it infinitely more satisfying. The beauty of mindful eating is that it enables you to tune into your hunger and fullness cues, reducing the chance of overeating.

Next, let's delve into the significance of knowing the origins of your food and the energy it imbues you with. After all, as the old saying goes—you are what you eat. Is the meat on your plate a product of an overcrowded factory farm pumped with steroids, hormones, and antibiotics? Or did it lead a free-range life on an organic farm? Are your fruits and vegetables GMO-filled, pesticide-drenched produce? It's time to ask the tough questions. "Is this food beneficial for my body? Does it nourish my soul and mind? Does this food reciprocate my love for it?" Your intuition is your best guide here; it intuitively knows what's best for you.

In the grander scheme of things, what we choose to eat affects us and the world around us. The environmental footprint of our dietary choices is indeed profound. As we continue our food journey, it's critical to consider the impact our plates have on the planet we call home. Livestock farming, for instance, is responsible for a substantial chunk of greenhouse gas emissions, not to mention the deforestation it causes and the enormous amounts of water it requires. On the other hand, plant-based foods require less land and water and produce fewer emissions. So by choosing to eat more plant-based foods, you're not just doing your health a favor; you're also contributing to the well-being of our planet.

It's not about perfection but about making conscious choices when and where you can. Think hearty vegetable stews, vibrant stir-fries, creamy avocado toasts, or even a decadent vegan chocolate cake. Every small step towards a more sustainable diet counts. So the next time you're in the supermarket, why not reach for the locally grown apples instead of the imported ones, or opt for the oat milk next to the dairy? Remember that your food choices have the potential to shape not just your health but also the health of our beautiful planet.

Shifting gears, let's contemplate the ways in which food enhances your life. Healthy eating isn't just about feeling good; it's about looking good and having a zest for life. Imagine the adventurous activities you could indulge in when your body is nourished by wholesome foods. The possibilities are limitless!

Finally, let's not forget the importance of gratitude in this entire process. Cultivating a sense of appreciation for the food we eat isn't just about saying "thank you" before a meal. It's about utterly understanding and appreciating the journey each morsel of food takes from the farm to our plates. Every grain, every leafy green, every succulent piece of fruit has a story of labor, love, and natural wonders behind it.

Imagine a simple apple. Think about the seed that was planted on the earth, the soil that nourished it, and the rain and sun that enabled it to grow. Consider the farmer who tended to the apple tree, the workers who carefully harvested the fruit, and the people involved in transporting it to your local store. Each apple is a testament to the miracles of nature and human effort.

Gratitude also extends to the preparation of our meals. Whether it's a quick snack you whipped up yourself, a feast cooked by a loved one, or even a meal prepared by a chef you've never met at a restaurant—time, skill, and resources have gone into creating the dish that's in front of you.

When we express gratitude for our food, we acknowledge and appreciate all these elements. We're honoring the earth, the people, and the processes involved in our sustenance. But gratitude doesn't just make our meals more meaningful; it can also make them more enjoyable. Studies have shown that expressing gratitude can heighten our senses, improving our food's taste. It can also slow down our eating process, aiding digestion, and absorption of nutrients.

Before your next meal, take a moment to express genuine appreciation for the food you're about to consume. You could say a few words of thanks, mentally acknowledge your food's journey or simply take a moment of silence to feel grateful. This simple act can transform your relationship with food and make each meal a celebration of life's abundance.

Wrapping up this exploration of mindful eating, it's clear that this practice offers a transformative approach to our relationship with food. Rather than rushing through meals or eating on autopilot, mindful eating invites us to make each meal a sensory experience, a moment of gratitude, and a form of self-care. It encourages us to honor the journey our food has taken from the earth to our plates and to consider the nourishment it offers us.

The beauty of mindful eating is that it's not just about what we eat but how we eat. It's about slowing down, tuning in, and truly savoring our food. It's about making conscious choices to support our health, respecting the environment, and contributing to a more sustainable and compassionate world.

With mindful eating, mealtime becomes meditation time. We turn off distractions and allow ourselves the time to engage with and enjoy our meals fully. We appreciate and express gratitude for the nourishment our food provides, not just for our bodies but also our minds and spirits. We engage all our senses, taking the time to appreciate our food's colors, smells, flavors, and textures.

Let's bring mindful eating to life. Take a moment to plan a meal and set aside dedicated time to fully embrace mindful eating. As you engage in this nourishing experience, incorporate the following mindfulness practice. Keep in mind that these steps are intended to be flexible guidelines rather than rigid rules, empowering you to cultivate a deeper connection with your food and the present moment:

Take a moment to observe: What different shapes, textures, and colors are on your plate?

*Looking at my plate, I notice it has*______________________________

____

Engage your sense of smell: What fruits, vegetables, and spices can you smell?

*When I take a deep breath, I can smell*__________________________

____

Savor the flavors: What flavors and spices can you taste on the tip of your tongue?

*As I take my first bite, I can taste*______________________________

____

Experience the textures: What does the food feel like in your mouth? How does the texture change as you chew it?

*The texture of this food in my mouth feels like*____________________

Listen: What noise does the food make as you bite into it?

*When I bite into this food, it sounds like*_________________________

____

____

Consider the journey of your food: Where did the food come from? Where did it grow? Is it organic? Has it been treated with pesticides, steroids, hormones, or antibiotics?

*I know that this food came from*________________________ *It was grown in*

____.

It is/is not organic.

It has/has not been treated with pesticides, steroids, hormones, or antibiotics.

Impact on your environmental footprint: How does your food consumption impact the earth, and what can you do to make it more sustainable?

When I think about the environmental footprint of my meals, I realize that

____

____

Tune into your feelings: Is this food good for my body? Is this food good for my soul? Is this food good for my mind? Does this food love me back? By eating this food now, how will I feel tomorrow?

*When I think about how this food affects my body, I feel*__________________

____

*This food nourishes my soul by*______________________________________

*When I eat this food, my mind feels*__________________________________

*This food shows love for me by*______________________________________

*If I eat this food now, tomorrow, I might feel*____________________________

Reflect on your goals: Does this food support your goals? How will this food enhance your life?

*This food supports my goals because*______________________________

____

*Eating this food will enhance my life by*___________________________

____

Trust your intuition: Deep down, what do you intuitively know is good for your body?

*Deep down, I know that this food is good/not good for me because*________

____

Know when to stop. It is advised to stop eating when you are 80 percent full or when it becomes unpleasant. How will you know when to stop eating?

*When I'm eating mindfully, I stop eating when*_______________________

____

As you embrace these steps, remember that mindful eating is a journey rather than a destination. Each meal is a new opportunity to practice mindfulness, make conscious choices, and nourish yourself in the most profound sense. Happy mindful eating!

24

Healthy Detox

"Detoxing is like having an internal party for your body's cells. They're dancing, detoxing, and thanking you for finally giving them the VIP treatment they deserve."

-Anonymous

The Marvel of Internal Housekeeping

Imagine your body as a bustling city, teeming with activity at all hours. Amidst the hustle and bustle, a diligent, tireless team is working behind the scenes—the detoxification crew. Their mission? To keep the city clean and habitable, combating the constant influx of unwanted visitors—toxins we encounter daily. From the food we eat, the air we breathe, to the products we use, our bodies are ceaselessly battling elements that can compromise our well-being if not promptly dismissed. This is where the role of detoxification takes center stage.

Detoxification, in essence, is your body's version of an extensive spring cleaning. It's a process that champions the expulsion of harmful substances or toxins, paving the way for a healthier, more vibrant you. The body naturally wields this power through dedicated organs like the liver, kidneys, skin, lungs, and digestive system. However, in today's world, with our bodies being bombarded by an astonishing number of toxins, our internal cleaning crew could use some reinforcements.

Regularly engaging in detoxification rituals can provide this much-needed support, bolstering our natural detox processes and facilitating more efficient toxin removal. By sweeping out the toxins and then replenishing your body with wholesome nutrients, detoxification can fortify your defenses against diseases and rejuvenate your ability to maintain optimal health.

But detoxification isn't just a tale of expulsion; it's also a story of renewal and nourishment. It's a holistic narrative that sees you, the protagonist, in your entirety—body, mind, and spirit— striving for optimal health and wellness. It prompts you towards a healthier lifestyle, championing cleaner eating, regular exercise, and mindful practices that manage stress and enhance overall well-being.

The benefits of embarking on this detoxification journey are manifold, from the aesthetic rewards of clearer skin to the internal advantages of improved digestion, elevated energy levels, and mental clarity. More than that, it sets the stage for a narrative of healthier habits, inspiring you to make wiser food choices, engage in invigorate physical activity, and prioritize self-care—all contributing to your long-term health story.

In the upcoming sections, we'll explore the diverse detox rituals you can weave into the tapestry of your daily routine. These practices will aid in eliminating toxins, supercharging your body's natural detoxification systems, and ultimately, helping you author a healthier, more radiant life story.

Before we dive into the detox plan, it's important to identify and acknowledge the sources of toxins in the first place. There are numerous environmental toxins that are beyond our control. However, let's focus our energy on the ones we can control so that we can take proactive steps toward a healthier lifestyle.

- **Alcohol: The Detoxification Dilemma.**

One of the most effective ways to support a robust detoxification system is to limit or completely avoid alcohol. It's the liver's job to metabolize over 90 percent of consumed alcohol. When you drink excessively, this leads to fat accumulation, inflammation, and scarring in the liver. With a compromised liver, the crucial process of filtering waste and toxins from your body becomes a daunting task.

- **Sugar and Processed Food: The Unseen Enemies**

Sugary and heavily processed foods are your body's silent foes. They've been linked to chronic diseases like heart disease, cancer, and diabetes, which inhibit your body's natural detoxification abilities by damaging critical organs like the liver and kidneys. Rather than going for artificial sugars, opt for natural sweeteners found in whole foods like fruits, dates, and pure maple syrup. Prioritize real food, like whole grains, fruits, vegetables, beans, nuts, and seeds, and stay wary of processed items that come in packages with long, unrecognizable ingredient lists.

- **The Oil Crisis: Unlocking the Truth about Oils**

Oil can be a hidden source of toxicity. Certain oils, like vegetables, peanut, sunflower, cottonseed, and canola, can be harmful. opt for healthier oils such as extra-virgin olive oil, coconut oil, avocado oil, hemp oil, and flaxseed oil for a toxin-free alternative.

- **Skin Deep: Toxic Body Care Products**

As the largest organ, your skin absorbs everything you apply to it. So if an ingredient in your body care product isn't something you'd want in your stomach, it's probably not good for your skin. Consider switching to natural deodorants, moisturizers, shampoos, and makeup to reduce chemical exposure.

- **Endocrine Disruptor Products: The Hidden Threat**

While harmful to you and your body, endocrine disruptors also pose a significant threat to the Earth. Reducing the use of these products benefits your health and decreases your carbon footprint, contributing to a healthier planet. These compounds can disrupt your body's hormonal balance, leading to elevated levels of certain hormones and hampering their essential breakdown. Exposure to endocrine disruptors has been associated with many health issues, such as cancers, fertility issues, and congenital disabilities.

These disruptive agents are commonly found in plastic bottles, storage containers, food wraps, cosmetics, detergents, medicines, flame retardants, food, toys, and even pesticides. Aim to reduce your usage of plastic in cooking and storage, opt for natural cleaning products over commercial ones, use non-toxic herbicides, and prioritize organic products whenever possible.

> *"Detoxification is not a punishment; it's a gift you give yourself, a way to honor your body and promote optimal health from the inside out."*

When you hear the word 'detox,' you might think of a harrowing drug detox, a brutal alcohol detox, or even the dreaded wheatgrass enemas. But fear not, my friend. That's not the detox I'm talking about. I'm referring to simple, everyday actions you can take to eliminate toxins in your body and keep yourself running like a well-oiled, healthy, and energetic machine.

By removing excess toxins, you'll rev up your energy levels, balance your hormones, and keep yourself going strong throughout the day like a superhero. Detoxification can also help with long-term weight management by kicking those toxins to the curb that are meddling with proper metabolic function.

Let's embark on an invigorating journey of daily detox rituals. Here, we're not just talking about a quick fix but lasting lifestyle changes that will leave you feeling like a whole new person. Here are some daily detox rituals that can assist in setting you up with healthy habits and have you feeling like the detox champion of the world:

1. **Wakey, wakey, lemon and shaky:** Start your day with a glass of warm lemon water. It's like giving your insides a morning spa session. It helps to flush your digestive system and rehydrate your body.
2. **Apple Cider Vinegar, the underrated superstar:** Add one to two teaspoons to warm water before meals. It's like a detoxifying appetizer that helps digestion and alkalizes your body. ACV is like the Swiss army knife of detox—it also helps break up mucus and cleanse the lymph nodes.
3. **Dive into the water:** Not literally, but drink lots of it. Water detoxifies your body by acting as a waste management system, removing waste products through the triumvirate of elimination—urination, breathing, and sweating. Aim for half your body weight in ounces or play it safe and go for the classic eight glasses a day. And remember, always choose filtered water to avoid an unwanted dose of toxins.
4. **Join the antioxidant party:** Antioxidant-rich foods are like your body's personal security team, helping to fight against oxidative stress caused by excess free radicals and other toxins. So load up on berries, fruits, nuts, cocoa, vegetables, spices, and beverages like coffee and green tea.
5. **Become a fiber fanatic:** High-fiber foods are the ticket to a clean and happy gut. Fiber acts like a sponge, soaking up toxins and escorting them out of your body via the toilet express. So pile on those organically grown fresh fruits, vegetables, grains, and brown rice.
6. **Teatime, Detox Edition:** Green tea and Herbal teas like dandelion root, burdock, milk thistle, chamomile, and turmeric can transform your liver into a detox powerhouse. These teas are like your liver's personal cleaning crew, helping cleanse and protect it.

7. **Prebiotics and Probiotics, the dynamic duo:** Prebiotics feed the good bacteria in your gut, while probiotics ensure everything moves through the system and is eliminated effectively. It's like having an efficient waste management system right in your gut. Foods rich in prebiotics include bananas, asparagus, onions, garlic, and oats. Probiotics are found in yogurt and fermented foods like kombucha, miso, kimchee, and sauerkraut.
8. **Spice up your life:** Cilantro, ginger, hot pepper, and coriander not only add a kick to your dishes but aid digestion and eliminate heavy metals. They're like your body's personal spice superheroes, fighting off toxins with each bite.
9. **Tongue Scraping, the unsung hero:** Clean your tongue of accumulated bacteria and debris from the night before. It's like giving your mouth a fresh start every morning.
10. **Get moving:** Exercise is not simply good for your waistline but also for reducing inflammation and aiding detoxification. Remember that sweating is your body's natural way of releasing toxins, so embrace it!
11. **Breathe deeply:** Breathing exercises can help cleanse the respiratory system and oxygenate the blood. Each deep breath is like a mini detox session for your lungs.
12. **Yoga, a workout, and detox in one:** Certain yoga poses can help release built-up toxins by massaging our organs. It's like giving your body an internal massage.
13. **Dry-brush the toxins away:** This gentle exfoliating massage technique, done with a soft bristle brush, is like a wake-up call for your lymphatic system. Start at the tips of your toes and fingers and work towards your heart, activating your blood circulation and detoxifying your skin. It's your body's natural spa treatment!
14. **Soak it up with Epsom Salt:** An Epsom salt bath is like a magic potion that draws out toxins, eases stress, improves sleep, and feels

fantastic on sore muscles after a workout. It's a detox in disguise as a relaxing soak in the tub!

15. **Hydrotherapy, your shower routine reimagined:** Why not amp up your shower routine after dry brushing? Alternate hot and cold showers to increase circulation, encourage lymphatic flow, and boost metabolism and immune function. Think of it as your personal waterfall, rejuvenating your body one drop at a time!
16. **Castor Oil Pack Massage, a detoxifying belly rub:** Castor oil stimulates the liver and colon, playing a crucial role in detoxification. When absorbed, it increases lymphocytes and speeds up the removal of toxins from your tissues. To create a castor oil pack, rub a quarter-sized amount in a clockwise direction over your abdomen. Cover with an old towel, apply a hot water bottle or heat pack, and let it work its magic. The heat helps the oil penetrate the liver and intestines, stimulating their contraction and encouraging movement and release of toxins. It's like a detoxifying lullaby for your insides!
17. **Good Night's Sleep, the ultimate detox:** A good night's sleep allows your brain to reorganize, recharge, and remove toxic waste byproducts accumulated throughout the day. Think of it as your body's natural reset button. But remember, it's not just about quantity but quality. So limit that blue light exposure before bed, stick to a sleep schedule, and aim for a solid seven to nine hours of shut-eye each night. It's the dreamiest detox of all!

So there you have it, a treasure chest of daily detox rituals designed to have you feeling healthier, happier, and more energized. Remember that the road to health is not a sprint but a marathon. Take it one step at a time, one day at a time, and before you know it, you'll be crossing that finish line, feeling like a million bucks!

Which three detox rituals do you see yourself integrating into your daily routine?

1. ______________________________

2. ______________________________

3. ______________________________

How can you alter your eating habits to reduce toxin intake?

*To decrease my toxin intake, I can modify my diet by*______________

____

____

How do you reduce your exposure to environmental toxins?

*I minimize my exposure to environmental toxins by*______________

____

____

Consider the personal care products you use daily. Which ones may have harmful ingredients?

The personal care products I use that may contain harmful ingredients are

____

What changes can you make to your skincare and beauty routine to avoid exposure to harmful chemicals?

*To reduce exposure to toxic chemicals, I can change my skincare and beauty routine by*______________________________

____

What steps can you take to reduce exposure to endocrine disruptors in your daily life?

*To reduce my exposure to endocrine disruptors, I will*____________________

____

What actions can you take to decrease your alcohol consumption for a healthier lifestyle?

To reduce my alcohol consumption, I will ____________________________

____

How do you plan to maintain a toxin-free lifestyle in the long run?

To support a toxin-free lifestyle, I commit to _________________________

____

Detoxification isn't a punishment; it's a gift you give yourself—an opportunity to honor your body and nurture optimal health from the inside out. These daily detox rituals serve as a roadmap, guiding you toward sustainable lifestyle changes. As you incorporate these practices into your daily routine, you'll experience the transformational rewards of feeling revitalized and ready to embrace each day as the author of your own health and wellness journey.

25

Harmonizing Your Home

"Create a sanctuary of balance and harmony in your surroundings, where serenity becomes the backdrop for your everyday life."

-Anonymous

A journey towards inner peace and outer order

Let me tell you about my dear friend, whom I will refer to as Lisa. Lisa is a force of nature—a vibrant and passionate individual with a twinkle in her eye and a contagious zest for life. She's the kind who dives headfirst into new adventures and embraces every opportunity for growth and self-discovery. However, beneath her radiant exterior, Lisa was secretly battling a persistent feeling of being overwhelmed and disconnected from her inner joy. Little did she know that a life-changing transformation was about to unfold, starting with a simple decision that would lead her on a journey of decluttering and rediscovery.

One day, as Lisa was rummaging through her overflowing closet, she stumbled upon a pair of jeans she swore she had lost five years ago. Amazed at her forgetfulness, she chuckled and thought, "Well, it seems like my closet has turned into a time capsule!"

Amidst the laughter and fashion time travel, Lisa realized that her cluttered home had become a reflection of her chaotic mind. She knew it was time to bring order and simplicity back into her life. She couldn't help but wonder if decluttering her space would also help her find that missing sock, she lost ages ago.

Inspired by the thought of organized drawers and an end to missing socks, Lisa made a decision—it was time to declutter and transform her home. She yearned for a sanctuary where she could find her favorite things without digging through a mountain of "stuff" that seemed to have a life of its own.

Lisa donned her decluttering cape and grabbed a sturdy trash bag. She started in the kitchen, saying a heartfelt goodbye to all the outdated appliances that had never mastered the art of evenly toasting bread.

Lisa encountered countless forgotten treasures and oddities as she made her way through each room. She discovered a collection of mismatched socks in a dark corner of the laundry room and set them free, hoping they'd find their missing partners in sock heaven.

With each item she tossed into the donation pile, Lisa could practically hear her home breathe a sigh of relief. It was as if the walls were saying, "Finally, we can breathe!"

As the clutter dissipated, Lisa felt a sense of liberation and clarity. She marveled at the newfound space and the lightness that enveloped her home. It was like an invisible Feng Shui guru had sprinkled magic decluttering dust around her.

But the real magic happened within Lisa herself. She discovered that decluttering wasn't just about tidying up physical spaces; it was a transformative journey of self-discovery. With each item she let go of, she released old attachments and made room for new possibilities.

As she shared her decluttering adventures with her friends, they laughed at the absurdities they found buried in the depths of their closets. They swapped stories of lost treasures and the joy of letting go. Lisa realized that decluttering wasn't just about creating a serene home but cultivating a lighter, more joyful way of living.

Disclaimer Note: The client story presented above is a fictionalized composite of experiences from multiple clients I have worked with. Names, identifying details, and specific circumstances have been changed to protect their privacy. While this story is not about an actual individual, it is rooted in the struggles, triumphs, and transformative journeys that many of my clients have experienced.

So my friend, as you embark on your decluttering journey, remember Lisa's story and giggle as you bid farewell to mismatched socks and random trinkets that have overstayed their welcome. Embrace the opportunity to reclaim your space, rejuvenate it, and create a home that brings a smile to your face.

Let's dive deeper into the ways you can declutter, organize, and discover the joy of simplicity and the freedom that comes from surrounding yourself with things that truly spark joy. Get ready to declutter your space, declutter your mind, and create a home that reflects your unique spirit and uplifts your soul.

Give yourself permission to invest the time and effort needed to make your home a place where you genuinely want to be. Returning home, decompressing, and finding tranquility in a disorderly, cluttered environment can be challenging. Embrace the opportunity to reclaim your space, rejuvenate it, and create a home that you genuinely love living in.

Time to Tidy Up

A cluttered home can feel like a chaotic jungle where misplaced treasures lurk in every corner. But fear not, for tidying up can transform your space into a peaceful sanctuary that nurtures your mind, body, and soul.

Our environment is like a mirror, reflecting our mental state. Picture yourself in a pristine kitchen, where you can whip up gourmet meals without the stress of a wild goose chase for utensils and ingredients. The power of tidiness is undeniable—it keeps pests at bay, reduces dust and allergens, and uplifts your overall well-being. So say goodbye to stress, anxiety, and depression as you bid farewell to clutter.

Don't let the idea of an enormous decluttering project overwhelm you.

It's time to channel your inner organizing guru and embrace the joy of tidying up one step at a time. Forget about striving for perfection; focus on taking small, consistent actions that lead to lasting change. Create a monthly plan that breaks down more significant tasks into manageable bites, and always remember to clean up after yourself daily.

Discover the organizing method that speaks to your soul—whether it's color-coding your wardrobe, arranging your pantry by food type, or turning your bookshelf into a work of art. Finding a system that resonates with you and fills your heart with joy is the secret to a tidy home.

As you embark on this journey toward a clutter-free haven, infuse your efforts with humor, wisdom, and inspiration. Laugh at the absurdity of that long-lost sock you finally found, learn from the ingenious storage solutions you stumble upon, and allow the transformation of your space to inspire your personal growth.

So go forth, declutter, and embrace the magic of a tidy home. You'll find that in the process, you're not only creating a harmonious living space but also nurturing your inner peace and cultivating a more joyful, inspired life.

- **Daily: Small steps, big impact**

Embrace the power of making your bed each morning. This seemingly insignificant act takes mere seconds and is a game-changer setting the tone for a productive day. Imagine the pride and motivation you'll feel, knowing you've already accomplished something before your day has truly begun. Plus, sliding into a neatly made bed at night is a delightful treat that can improve your sleep quality.

Cultivate the habit of putting things away after using them, and gently part ways with items that no longer serve you. For example, keep your bathroom pristine by returning your toothbrush, makeup, and hair care products to their rightful homes. Turn meal cleanup into a mindful ritual by washing dishes, putting them away, and wiping down counters.

Before bedtime, invest ten minutes in a quick home tidy-up. Straighten each room, put clothes and toys in their designated spots, and let your home breathe a sigh of relief. By tidying up the night before, you will wake up to a fresh, welcoming space where your day can unfold smoothly—no more tripping over toys or wrestling with a cluttered kitchen sink.

- **Weekly Wonders: Fair chore distribution and domestic harmony**

Set aside at least an hour each week for household chores like vacuuming, mopping, dusting, and scrubbing. If you share your living space with others, ensure everyone chips in to avoid any Cinderella-esque resentment.

- **Monthly Magic: Declutter and rejuvenate.**

Once a month, dedicate four hours to tackling more extensive projects, such as organizing closets, washing windows, or sprucing up your garage. As you purge the clutter, remember to part ways with items that no longer bring you joy or serve a purpose in your life. Channel your inner Marie Kondo and thank these belongings for their service before letting them go.

By incorporating these daily, weekly, and monthly habits, you'll create a serene, clutter-free sanctuary that nurtures your mind, body, and soul. So start today, and watch as your life blossoms with the magic of a tidy, harmonious home.

Do any beliefs or thoughts keep you from creating an organized living space? Are there any specific areas in your home that you find challenging to keep organized? If so, why?

The areas in my home that I find challenging to keep organized are ________

____________________________ *because*________________________________

____

How can you motivate yourself to maintain a clean and organized environment consistently?

To motivate myself to maintain a clean and organized environment, I will

____

____

How can you involve family members or roommates in maintaining a clean and organized living space?

I will involve family members or roommates in maintaining a clean-living space by ______________________________________

____

____

Can you identify any habits or routines that contribute to clutter or disorganization? How can you change or replace them?

One habit or routine that contributes to clutter is ______________, *and I will change or replace it by*______________________________

____

Are there any tools, techniques, or resources you would like to explore to help you create and maintain a more organized living space?

To help create and maintain a more organized living space, I would like to explore ______________________________________

____

How do you feel about cultivating a healthy, organized, clean environment?

I feel ____

Have you noticed a connection between your environment and your mental state?

When my home feels cluttered, my thoughts tend to be ______________

When my home feels clean, my thoughts usually are ________________

List at least five ways living in a clean, organized environment can benefit you.

1. ____
2. ____
3. ____
4. ____
5. ____

What daily tidying tasks can you commit to?

Every day, I will ______________________________________

____

What weekly cleaning tasks can you commit to?

Each week, I will ______________________________________

____

____

What big projects are you committed to taking on to clean, organize, and declutter each month?

January, I will ______________________________

____

February, I will ______________________________

____

March, I will ______________________________

____

April, I will ______________________________

____

May, I will ______________________________

____

June, I will ______________________________

____

July, I will ______________________________

____

August, I will ______________________________

____

September, I will ______________________________

____

October, I will ______________________________

____

November, I will ____

____

December, I will ____

____

The power to transform your living space and, in turn, your life lies in your hands. By choosing to tidy up and maintain a clean and organized environment, you are enhancing your physical surroundings and taking a stand for your mental and emotional well-being.

Allow the serenity of a clutter-free environment to be a metaphor for the order, balance, and peace you seek within yourself. Embrace the joy that comes from knowing every corner of your home is a reflection of the vibrant, thriving, and harmonious individual you are.

Tidying up may not be an easy task, but the rewards are immeasurable. A clean and organized living space will energize you, foster creativity, and enable you to truly live in the present moment. Let today be the day you commit to change, the day you rise above the chaos and declare, "I am ready to create a sanctuary that reflects my highest self!"

Every small step you take brings you closer to the vision of the harmonious home and life you desire. So let the power of transformation ignite within you, inspiring not just the messiest of individuals but anyone who has ever dreamt of a better way of living. It's time to embark on this journey of self-discovery and self-care through the simple yet profound act of tidying up.

It's time to rise above chaos, embrace the beauty of a clean and organized environment, and unlock your true potential. You have the power within you to transform your living space into a sanctuary of peace, serenity, and inspiration. So take a deep breath, roll up your sleeves, and let the magic begin!

Transform your home into a sanctuary that reflects your unique spirit and uplifts your soul. Let's dive deeper into the ways you can create a joyful, serene, and inspiring haven.

- **Illuminate your home with nature's glow.**

Open the curtains and let the sun's vibrant energy fill your home. Natural light not only lifts your mood and enhances productivity but also supports your body in producing Vitamin D and improving your circadian rhythms and sleep patterns. The sun's rays are like free therapy, so go ahead and soak up that golden goodness. Remember that a little sunlight can turn a gloomy room into a cheerful oasis.

- **Infuse your space with the vitality of nature!**

Houseplants are nature's way of giving you a high-five. Not only do they purify the air and bring a sense of freshness to your space, but they also offer remarkable health benefits.

Choose plants that match your personality— maybe a sassy snake plant or a charming Ivy. Their vibrant presence can boost your mood, spark creativity, reduce stress, and even improve physical health. Plus, talking to your plants is a fantastic way to help them grow and boost you psychologically.

- **Designate spaces with purpose.**

Creating specific zones for various activities can help you find balance and focus. For example, reserving your bed solely for sleep and relaxation will improve the quality of your rest. Even in a small living space, you can create designated areas for work, exercise, cooking, eating, and sleeping. It's all about embracing your inner interior designer and channeling that positive energy into functional spaces.

- **Choose meaningful decoration over clutter.**

Display artwork and decorations that evoke positive energy and align with the purpose of each room. Maybe a motivational quote in your office, a whimsical painting in the living room, or even a hilarious fridge magnet that makes you smile every time you open the refrigerator. Thoughtful placement of inspirational pieces can uplift your mood and create harmony in your environment, while decluttering frees up space for spontaneous dance parties.

- **Carve out your personal Zen zone.**

Create a unique haven dedicated to meditation, yoga, reading, or journaling in your home. This sacred space, whether an entire room, a cozy reading nook, or a corner adorned with crystals and a meditation cushion, should house the spiritual tools that resonate with your true self and help you connect with a higher power. It's your personal retreat, so make it a place where you feel inspired, peaceful, and ready to unleash your inner superhero.

Ponder the steps you're willing to take to transform your home into a sanctuary where you can find solace and rejuvenation:

*I will create a tranquil living space by*______________________________

____

____

Now, go forth with determination, knowledge, and inspiration to create a living space that nurtures your body, mind, and spirit. Embrace the challenge, and let the magic of a clean, organized, and harmonious environment unfold before your eyes.

26

Rewilding your life

"Wellness is essentially being in tune with Nature and aligning ourselves with the inherent wisdom within us all."

-Anonymous

Dancing with the Rhythm of Life

There's profound wisdom that lies within the heart of Nature, whispering the secrets of wellness and harmony to those who pause to listen. We are intrinsically woven into the fabric of the natural world, and by embracing our connection to Nature, we align ourselves with the inherent wisdom that resides within us all.

Why connect with Nature? Simply because Nature nurtures our well-being, as we are a part of it. Spending time in Nature can bring feelings of peace and serenity, significantly reduce stress, and act as an anti-inflammatory. Our bodies comprise all the same elements, minerals, and energy that make up the planet, so it makes perfect sense that the outer universe reflects our consciousness and our body. For instance, the percentage of water on Earth mirrors the same percentage of water in our bodies, and so on.

Despite our natural origins, it's all too easy to fall out of alignment with our true selves.

Mentally, we disconnect from Nature as we deeply immerse ourselves in a human-made world. In this modern era, many of us live in an asphalt jungle surrounded by trains, planes, and skyscrapers, where we seldom see a blue sky, sink our hands into the earth, breathe in the fresh air, or walk barefoot on the grass. We can easily get caught up in the rat race of life, forgetting to be human beings rather than merely human doers.

Let me share with you a little story that serves as a reminder of our connection to Nature:

Once upon a time, a young woman named Maya was in a bustling city. Every day, she would rush through her daily tasks, barely stopping to take a breath. She was always on the go, never really noticing the beauty of the world around her. Then, one day, as she was walking through a park on her way to work, she stumbled upon a hidden garden. Curiosity piqued; she ventured inside.

In the garden, she found vibrant flowers, towering trees, and a gentle breeze that carried the sweet scent of blossoms. She heard birds singing and felt the soft grass beneath her feet. It was as if time stood still, and for the first time in years, she felt a deep sense of peace and connection to the world around her.

As the days went by, Maya began to visit the garden regularly, allowing herself to reconnect with Nature and remember the wisdom of her true self. She discovered that by embracing the beauty and harmony of the natural world, she could bring balance and serenity into her own life. And so with each visit to the garden, Maya's spirit blossomed, and she became a beacon of light, inspiring others to seek the healing power of Nature.

So dear friend, I invite you to take a step back from the chaos of life, break free from the chains of the human race, take a leap into Nature's embrace, and become a human "being." Begin the journey of being a human being once again, and revel in the connection and inspiration that Nature provides. Let the wisdom of the natural world guide you, and may you always remember to nurture your bond with the Earth that sustains all of us.

As you embark on this journey to reconnect with Nature and rediscover the wisdom within, let us turn to the words of an ancient Ojibway prayer that speaks to the heart of our mission. This prayer calls upon the guidance of the Sacred One to help us heal ourselves and the Earth by learning love, compassion, and honor. Let us reflect on these powerful words:

Grandfather,
Look at our brokenness,
We know that in all creation
Only the human family
Has strayed from the sacred way.
We know that we are the ones
Who are divided
And we are the ones
Who must come back together
To walk in the sacred way
Grandfather,
Sacred One,
Teach us love, compassion, and honor That we may heal the earth
And heal each other.

-Ojibway prayer

As the Ojibway prayer resonates within us, let it serve as a gentle reminder to embrace our innate connection with the natural world. It's time to commit to nature, allowing it to nourish and heal us, just as we seek to heal the Earth. Through our mindful actions, we can rediscover the beauty and solace that the great outdoors has to offer, and in doing so, we can find harmony within ourselves and our environment. Let us heed the call of the Sacred One and embark on a journey of reconnection and commitment to nature, enriching our lives and the world around us.

Commitment to Connect with Nature

- **Create time alone in Nature**

Nature always has time for you—it's like a friend who's always there for you 24/7! There is no need to schedule an appointment or save a date with Nature. It's available any time of day or night. So pencil in some quality time with your green pals.

Which days of the week and times can you commit to spending quality time in nature?

I commit to spending quality time in nature every ____________________

____

- **Find an excellent place to surround yourself with Nature**

Take a hike in the forest, find a lake, ocean, or stream to dip your toes in, or spend time in a vegetable or flower garden. Find an open field, watch the stars, sleep outside, or have a chat with the local squirrels. Nature is full of incredible locations for your next adventure!

Where will you go to surround yourself with nature?

The places I can go to wrap myself in nature are ______________________

____

- **Sit or lie down on the earth and get cozy**

Relax and observe Nature's soundtrack and critters. Lay down, feel the heartbeat of the earth, and let your senses run wild! See the colors and shapes, listen to the sounds, feel with your entire body, smell everything, and taste nature's bounty of fruits and vegetables.

- **Converse with your leafy or furry friends**

Talk to Nature. It has no ego, will never judge you, and can be quite the conversationalist! Trust your inner feelings, pictures, and thoughts you receive; they are Nature's way of communicating. When you connect with Nature, you become one with the eternal show, harmonizing with your world.

- **Memorize the sounds and sights.**

Immerse yourself in the present moment and shut out all distractions that fill your busy mind. All of the natural sights and sounds are more than therapy; it's a connection, a link to your soul and the boundless creative energy of the universe.

- **Appreciate Nature**

Have gratitude towards Nature. Give thanks every time you are refreshed by its water, eat its delicious foods, and enjoy any part of it. Thank it over and over again. Have an abundance of gratitude for the many blessings it has given you and will continue to give you.

- **Take care of Nature and give back to it.**

Be conscious of your environmental footprint, the things you release into the earth. How are your choices affecting the environment? Clean up garbage and graffiti when you see it, even if it's not yours. Feel the plants' and animals' appreciation as you free them from trash and litter. Take part in creating more Nature by planting a garden or a tree. Together, we can nurture our world and help it flourish.

Reflect on your experiences connecting with Nature and the messages & lessons you've received:

What visual delights did you experience during your nature connection?

I saw ____

____

What symphony of sounds played in your ears while in nature?

I heard ____

____

What fragrances filled the air, and what did they remind you of?

I smelled ____

It reminded me of _____________________________________

What textures did you explore, and how did they feel?

I touched ____

It felt ____

Did you savor any flavors from nature? Describe the taste.

I tasted ____

It tasted like ____

What messages or insights did you gain from your time in nature?

The insights I learned are ______________________________

____

____

What aspects of nature do you honor, appreciate, and feel grateful for?

I am grateful for ____

____

____

What blessings or gifts did you discover in nature?

In nature, I found ____

____

How do you plan to care for and nurture nature daily?

I will care for nature by ____

____

Aligning with Your Circadian Rhythm

Did you know that our bodies are like finely tuned orchestras, playing the symphony of life in harmony with the universe's grand concert? It's true, and our circadian rhythm is the maestro that conducts this magical music within us. Our maestro, however, is a bit of a sun worshipper. It thrives when we live by the cycles of daylight and darkness.

Like all of Nature's wonders, our bodies operate on circadian rhythms. This means we have internal clocks that synchronize with the sun's rising and setting. Think of it as nature's way of setting a perfect rhythm for the 'dance of life. Every morning, as the sun rises, your body is ready to take on the world—work, exercise, eat, and during the evening, when the sun sets, your body starts winding down, preparing for a night of rest and recovery.

The maestro within us, our circadian rhythm, conducts various bodily functions, releasing hormones, adjusting body temperature, and controlling metabolism to keep us alert or guide us to sleep, all based on the environment's cues.

Just as a sensitive artist, our maestro doesn't react well to disturbances—ignoring your circadian rhythm is like trying to play a guitar with a spoon. The result might be weight gain, insomnia, fatigue, a decline in productivity, and even changes in mental health. But don't worry; you won't have to quit your night job or move into a cave to get back in rhythm.

You can realign with your natural rhythm by developing simple daily routines that revolve around the sun. It's like tuning your guitar before a performance or stretching before a marathon. You want to be in harmony with the rhythm of life. So here's a challenge—try living more aligned to your natural circadian rhythm for a month. See the difference it makes. And remember that the goal is not to become a circadian rhythm fanatic but to dance a little more with the rhythm of life. The maestro is ready, are you?

- **Restrict eating to sunlight hours**

Our bodies are hardwired to the rhythms of nature. The circadian rhythm, a 24-hour internal clock that governs our sleep-wake cycle, regulates various other physiological processes, including digestion and metabolism. Aligning our eating patterns with circadian rhythms can profoundly impact our health and well-being.

The idea behind restricting eating to daylight hours, also known as time-restricted eating or intermittent fasting, is to eat in sync with our body's natural circadian rhythm. As a result, we optimize our body's ability to process food and absorb nutrients, improve our sleep quality, and support our overall health.

Our bodies are designed to digest and assimilate food most efficiently during daylight hours when our metabolism is most active. In contrast, our metabolism slows down at night, preparing our bodies for rest and repair. Eating late into the evening or night can disrupt this natural rhythm, leading to imbalances and health issues over time.

Moreover, our insulin sensitivity is higher during the day, meaning our bodies can process carbohydrates more effectively, reducing the risk of weight gain and diabetes. Night-time eating has been linked to a higher risk of obesity, as our bodies are less efficient at processing food at this time.

By restricting eating to daylight hours, you're not just following a dietary trend but also aligning with your body's natural rhythms, optimizing your health. And yes, you may potentially drop a few pounds in the process!

In what ways can restricting eating to daylight hours benefit you?

Restricting eating to daylight hours can benefit me in several ways. For instance,

____,

and not to forget ______________________________________.

It could also lead to ____________________________________.

What does your eating window look like now?

Currently, I tend to start eating at ____________________ *and finish at* __________________

How does eating during this time window affect you?

This kind of eating schedule affects me in specific ways. For example, I've noticed that ______________________________________

____

What do you feel is a healthy eating window for you?

In my view, a healthy eating window for me would be from __________ *to* ____________*. I believe this because* ____________________

____

How can you slowly transition to this eating window? (Example: In the first two weeks, aim to eat between 8 a.m. and 8 p.m. Then, in the subsequent week, narrow it down to 8 a.m. to 7 p.m. and so on, until the desired eating window is reached.)

To transition to this eating window, I plan to take gradual steps starting with ____

____

What healthy changes can you make to your eating window starting today?

As for the healthy changes I can make starting today, I will ____________

____

Another change could be ______________________________

Remember that it's not just about squeezing the meals into a tighter window but also about mindful eating. Ensure that your meals are balanced and nutritious. Your body is like a grand symphony; food is the music that keeps it harmoniously flowing. Let's not play it out of tune! And hey, here's a fun fact—did you know that your gut has its own little clock, known as the gut clock? It's like an internal dinner bell, telling your body when it's time to digest and when it's time to take a break. So let's respect that bell and keep our meals timely! Your body is brighter than the latest diet fad. Listen to it, respect it, and it'll reward you with health and vitality. Here's to a healthier, brighter, and more energetic you!

- **Sync with the Sun for Better Health**

Once upon a time, before the invention of smartphones, artificial lights, and Netflix binges, people used to rise with the crowing of the rooster, work under the beaming sun, and call it a day when the twinkling stars started to fill the sky. Ah, those were the days, weren't they?

Fast forward to today, and it's a whole different ball game. We're more likely to rise to the sound of an annoying alarm clock, work under fluorescent lights, and end our days squinting at our screens in the wee hours of the night. Artificial light dominates our lives, and our bodies are crying out for a bit of sunshine!

Believe it or not, decreasing artificial light and spending more time outdoors under nature's spotlight can be a game-changer for your sleep quality and overall well-being. It's time to kick the indoorsy habit and go greet Mother Nature! The sun is waiting to shine on you, the flowers are ready to share their fragrance, and the birds are eager to serenade you. Why not start your day on a bright note? Catch the sunrise, take your morning coffee outdoors, or embark on a refreshing morning walk to get your daily dose of Vitamin D. Choose the window seat while working or dining. Let the sunlight wash over you, filling your day with warmth and energy.

As the sun begins to set, soak in the waning light. Step outside and let the dimming light signal your body that it's time to wind down. Bask in the evening hues of the sky and let the soothing tranquility prepare you for a restful night's sleep.

Remember friend, that balance is key. I'm not suggesting you give up your evening commitments, but I encourage you to seek opportunities to introduce more natural light into your daily life. So go ahead, seize the day, and let the sun light up your life!

Describe how your typical day starts.

My day usually begins by ____

How much natural light exposure do you usually get each day?

On a typical day, I spend ____

What activities do you do outside during daylight hours?

Some activities I enjoy in daylight are ________________________________

____

How can you incorporate more natural light into your daily routine?

To get more natural light, I will ____________________________________

____

How does spending time in natural light make you feel?

When I'm outdoors in the sunlight, I feel ______________________________

____

How do your energy levels and mood change with varying levels of natural light exposure?

I notice that when I get plenty of natural light, I _____________________

____

How can increasing your exposure to natural light affect your sleep quality?

I believe that more exposure to natural sunlight could __________________

____

Building a connection with nature, specifically daylight, is one of the simplest yet most profound steps we can take for our overall well-being. As you embrace the sunlight and sync your daily routines with the sun's schedule, you will notice a significant improvement in your energy levels, mood, and sleep quality. You'll find yourself more in tune with the natural world, and this harmony can also ripple into other aspects of your life.

Remember though, that the sun is a powerful force. While it can provide numerous health benefits, respecting its intensity is essential. Be mindful of how long you're in the sun, especially during peak hours when the rays are the strongest, and take appropriate precautions, such as wearing protective clothing and sunglasses to prevent any harm. So go ahead and step into the light—just remember to do it wisely!

- **Embrace the Night**

The essence of Cinderella's beautiful song reminds us that dreams are wishes from the heart during slumber. Cinderella's timeless tale underscores the significance of a good night's sleep. But let's face it—Cinderella didn't have to deal with the constant pinging of a smartphone, the glare of a late-night Netflix binge, or the relentless march of a 24/7 society. Today, the peaceful kingdom of sleep often feels under siege!

Let's debunk the myth that skimping on sleep is the badge of the uber-productive. Sleep isn't time wasted in the garage if we consider ourselves high-performance vehicles. Instead, it's the essential maintenance that keeps the engine purring. It recharges our bodies and resets our brains, consolidates memories, and prepares us for the learning and challenges of the day ahead.

"*Without enough sleep, we all become tall two-year-olds,*" JoJo Jensen wisely quipped. Aim for a restful, uninterrupted night of seven to nine hours, which is the golden range for adults. Did you know chronic sleep deprivation messes with the hormones controlling your appetite and metabolism, leading to weight gain? Or that it increases the risk of conditions like diabetes and heart disease? Yeah, it's not just about being grumpy in the morning.

Contrary to what the hustle culture promotes, compromising on sleep doesn't make us heroes; it makes us human-sized time bombs. The good news is with a consistent sleep routine and healthy habits, you can reclaim the night and wake up to days filled with energy, productivity, and overall well-being. So commit to prioritizing sleep and rediscovering the magic in a good night's rest. Trust me, your future bright-eyed, bushy-tailed self will thank you!

Think about sleep's impact on your daily life:

When I am well-rested, I notice that ______________________________

____

When I am sleep-deprived, I tend to ______________________________

____

My dear friend, as you embrace the dance of life, I want you to take a moment and recognize that this grand symphony isn't just our creation; it's a magnificent composition of which you are an indispensable part. Nature, in all its splendor, is your timeless teacher, imparting the wisdom of balance and harmony. In this journey, consider rewilding your life, for it's in the wild embrace of the natural world that you'll find profound connection and wisdom.

While you venture on this path of rediscovery, please remember your duty to nurture and safeguard the Earth, the very foundation of our existence. Listen to the whispers of the Sacred One, as echoed in the ancient Ojibway prayer, and strive to heal both yourself and our precious planet through love, compassion, and honor. By strengthening your bond with nature, you not only enrich your own life but also contribute to a brighter, more harmonious future for all living beings. As you waltz through nature's rhythm, let each step resonate with gratitude, reverence, and boundless love for the Earth and all its enchanting wonders.

27

Nighttime Navigation

"Finish each day before you begin the next and interpose a solid wall of sleep between the two. This you cannot do without temperance."

– Ralph Waldo Emerson

Your Guide to Harmonious Slumbers

In our hyperconnected, always-on society, it's easy to overlook the importance of preparing for sleep. With the hustle and bustle of the day often trailing into the night, it can be challenging to flip the switch and transition from wakefulness to sleep. That's where a bedtime ritual comes in.

A bedtime ritual is a set of relaxing activities performed in the same order, around the same time each evening, designed to cue your body that it's time to wind down and prepare for sleep. Just as the sun setting signals to the birds it's time to nest, your bedtime ritual signals to your body and mind that it's time to rest.

Creating an effective bedtime ritual can be likened to crafting a personal piece of art. It's a uniquely individual process, as what works well for one person may not work for another. However, despite its personal nature, there are fundamental principles that guide the process.

These principles include:

- **Blue Light Blues**

Our modern devices are like little digital sirens, luring us with entrancing blue light. But beware, this light can trick your body into thinking it's still daytime, disrupting your melatonin levels and making you toss and turn.

What steps can you take to combat these Blue Light Blues? First and foremost, consider setting a digital curfew for yourself. Aim to turn off all electronic devices at least an hour before bedtime to allow your body to prepare for sleep naturally.

If a digital curfew isn't feasible due to work or other commitments, explore other options, like using blue light filter settings on your devices. Many smartphones and laptops now come with 'night mode' settings, which reduce the amount of blue light emitted. Alternatively, consider investing in a pair of blue-light-blocking glasses, which can be worn in the evening to shield your eyes from disruptive light emissions.

In addition, make your bedroom a screen-free zone if possible. Not only can this reduce your exposure to blue light, but it can also help you mentally associate your bedroom with sleep rather than wakefulness and activity.

Remember that the goal is to establish a relaxing pre-bedtime routine that allows your body to wind down naturally. Reducing exposure to blue light in the evenings helps your body maintain its natural rhythm, setting the stage for a better night's sleep.

- **Cultivate Peaceful Moments for Better Sleep**

Dedicating some quiet moments to yourself before bed is essential to good sleep hygiene. Creating a bedtime ritual incorporating relaxing activities can signal to your mind and body that it's time to wind down, setting the stage for a restful night's sleep. Whether indulging in stargazing, losing yourself in a captivating book, or whispering sweet nothings to your beloved pet, finding a peaceful activity that resonates with you is key.

An evening routine emphasizing serenity and relaxation can bridge the day's stresses and the calm needed for a restful night's sleep. Such a routine can vary significantly based on individual preferences and lifestyle. Some might find tranquility through meditation or deep breathing exercises, while others might lean into journaling or enjoying soothing music.

Reading a book, for instance, is a favored bedtime activity that can significantly promote sleep. It offers an escape from daily concerns, transporting you to another realm. Likewise, gentle yoga or stretching can alleviate any physical tension accumulated over the day, setting your body up for relaxation.

Another relaxing activity could be taking a warm bath or shower. The rise and subsequent fall in body temperature can induce feelings of drowsiness. Combining this with the calming effects of water can make you feel incredibly relaxed and ready for bed.

Remember, the key is choosing activities you enjoy and look forward to. This way, your bedtime ritual becomes a pathway to better sleep and a cherished part of your day. It's all about finding what helps you transition from the hustle and bustle of your day to a state of serenity, preparing you for a restful, rejuvenating sleep.

- **Sleep's Frenemies; The Impacts of Caffeine, Alcohol, and Nicotine on Restful Nights**

Sleep is a delicate ballet, easily disrupted by the loud trumpets of stimulants like caffeine, alcohol, and nicotine. While these substances might be your go-to for energy boosts, stress relief, or social enjoyment, they can stealthily sabotage your sleep quality.

Take caffeine, the trusty ally against morning grogginess and afternoon slumps. This stimulating substance works by blocking adenosine, a neurotransmitter promoting sleep and relaxation. But as the day wears on, consuming caffeine can become a barrier to restful sleep. It lingers in your system for about five to six hours, meaning the afternoon coffee can keep you tossing and turning at night, preventing you from reaching the deep, restorative sleep stages.

Alcohol might seem like an excellent nightcap, a ticket to Dreamland. However, its initial sedative effects mask its true nature as a sleep disruptor. Alcohol suppresses REM sleep, which is crucial for memory, learning, and mood regulation. This interference leads to a "REM rebound" as your body attempts to catch up on this vital sleep stage, often resulting in increased dreams and nightmares. In addition, the muscle-relaxing effects of alcohol can exacerbate snoring and sleep apnea, and its diuretic properties may cause frequent nocturnal bathroom visits, further fragmenting your sleep.

Nicotine, the active compound in cigarettes and e-cigarettes, is another stimulant that can wreak havoc on your sleep. It makes falling asleep harder and disrupts the balance of sleep stages, leading to lighter, less restful sleep. As a muscle relaxant, it can intensify conditions like sleep apnea. Moreover, nicotine can disrupt your body's internal clock, leading to inconsistent sleep and waking patterns.

While caffeine, alcohol, and nicotine might offer temporary relief or enjoyment, they can compromise sleep quality. To nurture better, more restful sleep, consider moderating these substances. Limit caffeine consumption to earlier hours, avoid alcohol close to bedtime, and seek help if nicotine use affects your sleep. Navigating the impacts of these substances on sleep can be a crucial step towards healthier sleep patterns and overall well-being.

- **The Hidden Consequences of Mid-night Munchies**

Often, late-night snacking can feel like a secretive, indulgent encounter, a satisfying crunch in the quiet of the night, or a comforting nibble while you catch up on your favorite show. However, this nocturnal nibbling can become an uninvited guest in your quest for a restful night's sleep.

In the digestive aspect, when you eat, your body needs to work to process the food, breaking it down and absorbing the nutrients. This process requires energy and can leave your body in a state of alertness rather than relaxation. So when you eat close to bedtime, your body is kept awake, busily digesting instead of settling into sleep mode.

Moreover, late-night snacking, especially when it involves spicy or fatty foods, can lead to discomfort and conditions like heartburn or acid reflux. These conditions can cause significant discomfort and awaken you from your sleep, interrupting the restorative sleep cycles.

Therefore, if you're seeking better sleep quality, it's advisable to wrap up eating a few hours before your intended bedtime. This window allows your body ample time to digest your last meal, ensuring that your digestive processes don't interfere with your sleep cycles. The key is balance and timing—nourishing your body without compromising your rest. So next time, consider reaching for a restful night's sleep instead of reaching for that midnight snack.

- **Crafting Your Ideal Sleep Sanctuary**

The space where we sleep is pivotal in the quality of our rest. Think of your bedroom as a sanctuary, a sacred place dedicated to peace, tranquility, and sleep. This space's arrangement, comfort, and aesthetics can directly influence your ability to fall asleep swiftly and stay asleep throughout the night.

Start by decluttering your bedroom, then invest in comfortable bedding. Your mattress, pillows, and blankets should provide ample support and comfort. Consider the material of your sheets—breathable fabrics like cotton can help regulate your body temperature throughout the night.

Speaking of temperature, aim to keep your bedroom cool. The National Sleep Foundation suggests a bedroom temperature of about 65 degrees Fahrenheit for optimal sleep. Consider using a fan or air conditioning during warmer months and limiting heavy blankets in cooler months to maintain this temperature.

Lastly, pay attention to the sensory elements in your room. Dimming the lights before bed can signal to your body that it's time to rest. If possible, use blackout curtains or an eye mask to limit light exposure during the night. For some, adding white noise or calming sounds can also be beneficial.

- **Slumberland Schedule**

When you adhere to a regular sleep schedule, your body anticipates sleep and waking times. This can result in easier falling asleep at night and more natural waking in the morning. You're essentially 'training' your body to expect sleep at certain times, making the process smoother and more efficient.

On the contrary, irregular sleep patterns can disrupt your circadian rhythm and melatonin levels, the hormone that signals your brain it's time to relax and head to bed. This disruption can lead to difficulty falling asleep, frequent awakenings at night, and poorer sleep quality.

Consistency is key! Going to bed and waking up at the same time daily sends a powerful signal to your internal body clock, which can result in improved sleep and waking function. It's like composing a love letter to your circadian rhythm, respecting its natural ebb and flow, and reaping the benefits in return.

- **The Powerful Link Between Exercise and Sleep**

Regular exercise is not just for achieving your fitness goals or maintaining a healthy weight; it's also a powerful ally in promoting better sleep. Regular physical activity can help you fall asleep more quickly, improve the quality of your sleep, and extend its duration.

Physical activity reduces insomnia by decreasing arousal, anxiety, and depressive symptoms. In addition, it helps to regulate your body's internal 24-hour clock, your circadian rhythm. In people with insomnia, a moderate workout can increase the time spent in deep sleep.

Exercise can also help to alleviate anxiety and depressive symptoms, common culprits of sleep problems. Physical activity leads to the release of endorphins, your brain's feel-good neurotransmitters. This can result in an elevation of mood and a reduction in stress and anxiety, creating a better mental environment for sleep.

However, timing is crucial when it comes to exercising for better sleep. It's generally recommended to avoid vigorous exercise in the hours leading up to bedtime, as it can interfere with your ability to fall asleep. This is due to the stimulating effects of exercise, including increased heart rate and body temperature. Instead, aim for morning or early afternoon workouts, as this helps to reset your circadian rhythm and promotes natural, restful sleep.

By embracing these strategies, you're not just creating a bedtime routine; you're crafting a symphony of rest. Each element is a note that, when played together, harmonizes into a restful and rejuvenating slumber. Your barriers are just the sour notes in your symphony and are beatable. Identify them and find a way to hit the right notes.

As you embark on this journey towards better sleep, remember this—Sleep is not a luxury; it's a necessity. So bid farewell to counting sheep and say hello to quality sleep! After all, a well-rested you is the best you!

Take your time to explore each question and be as detailed as you can. This will help you create a more effective bedtime routine and better understand your sleep habits and needs.

Reflect on your current nighttime routine.

My current nighttime routine consists of ______________________________

____

Identify what you would like to change about your current routine.

I want to change ___________________ *about my current routine because.*

____

Think about a relaxing activity you enjoy doing before bed.

One relaxing activity I enjoy before bed is ___________________ *because.*

____

How can you limit exposure to screens and blue light before bedtime?

To limit my exposure to screens and blue light before bed, I will __________

____

What foods or drinks affect your sleep?

When I consume ___________________________ *before bed, I notice that*

____

What changes can you make to your bedroom to reflect comfort and calmness?

To create a more calming and restful environment in my bedroom, I will

____

____

How can you make your bedtime routine more consistent?

To make my bedtime routine more consistent, I plan to ________________

____

What benefits do you hope to gain from a new bedtime routine?

By creating a new bedtime routine, I hope to ______________________

____

What challenges might come up when implementing your new bedtime routine?

Some challenges that might arise when implementing my new routine could be ____

____

____

Plan out how you will deal with these challenges.

*To overcome these challenges, I will*______________________

____

____

Write out your new bedtime routine, incorporating the changes you've considered.

My new bedtime routine will be ______________________

____

____

____

____

____

Sleep can often take a backseat in the hustle and bustle of our modern world. However, it's time we reclaim our nights and embrace the regenerative power of rest. Remember that every good day starts the night before. So be kind to yourself by prioritizing sleep, setting boundaries, and creating a serene sleep environment. As you nurture your body with quality sleep, you'll reap the benefits in your waking hours with more energy, better focus, and overall well-being. So here's to sweet dreams and brighter days!

28

Rediscover Your Joy of Movement and Exercise

"Exercise is not punishment for what you ate; it's a celebration of what your body can do."

-Anonymous

The Fun-Filled Prescription for Daily Play

Does the word "exercise" bring to mind a scene of sweat-drenched hours spent lifting ungodly weights at a gym or perhaps an endless, Sisyphean journey on a treadmill? Likewise, you may visualize a monotonous regimen of squats, push-ups, lunges, and crunches. If these images get you pumped up, hats off to you, fitness aficionado! If not, don't sweat it (pun intended); you're in good company. The goal here is to move your body daily rather than train for the next Ironman.

Think of daily physical movement as nature's own magic pill, minus the tiny print of side effects. It's like a free gym membership, except this one is to Club Healthy Life! Regular exercise can boost your memory (so you'll remember where you put those pesky keys), enhance brain function (enabling you to solve crosswords faster), improve heart health (your heart will thank you), increase sleep quality (who doesn't love a good snooze?), and reduce joint stiffness (your knees will feel like they're twenty again!).

The list doesn't stop there! It's also a ticket to a longer, more fulfilled life, a shield against chronic diseases, a helper in weight management, a tool to lower blood pressure, and a natural mood enhancer to combat anxiety and depression. Plus, maintaining balance and muscle strength means you could join the circus as a tightrope walker if the mood takes you!

Now, a cautionary tale—We've all seen those glossy magazine covers featuring perfectly sculpted bodies, which have somehow fooled us into equating exercise with weight loss or pursuing the "perfect" body. This mindset, my friend, is as outdated as a flip phone. Exercise isn't just about weight loss—and, truth be told, it isn't necessary for it. Over-exercising can be like that friend who overstays their welcome – it can weaken your immune system and raise the risk of injuries, such as tendinitis and stress fractures.

Let's trade the grueling, joyless workouts for something that feels more like a dance party and less like a chore. It's time to shift your perspective on exercise and transform it into a joyful daily routine that nourishes your mind, body, and spirit. Remember that the best kind of exercise is the one that leaves you feeling refreshed, rejuvenated, and ready to take on the world, one step (or dance move) at a time!

Rethinking Exercise, From Chore to Joy. What are some fitness misconceptions you've held onto?

Once upon a time, I believed exercise was ______________________________

____

Now, let's flip the script and rewrite those old fitness narratives.

*From now on, I choose to see physical activity as*______________________

____

Here's some fantastic news that will inspire you, regardless of your physical limitations or capabilities, to embark on your exercise journey—There are no excuses when it comes to moving your body and embracing the power of simple exercise. Whether you have physical limitations or possess the ability to conquer Mount Everest, exercise is a universal opportunity for all.

It's true that the type of exercise you do doesn't matter as much as your commitment to showing up and embracing the movement. So, let's banish the notion that exercise is only for a select few or those with specific abilities. It's time to rewrite the narrative and prove you can find joy and fulfillment in physical activity.

Once upon a time, you were a child who found exercise without even looking for it because, back then, it was called 'play.' It was a time of carefree exploration and enjoyment. Remember effortlessly skipping around the house, sprinting on sun-kissed beaches, wrestling playfully with ocean waves, and engaging in an epic game of frisbee with your furry friend.

Those nights when you danced with reckless abandon, explored the heart of Mother Nature, reveled in outdoor games, pedaled your bike down picturesque lanes, or ruled the park with your roller skates.

Regardless of your physical capabilities, you can tap into that same spirit of playfulness and incorporate activities that bring you happiness and excitement. Whether it's a leisurely stroll in the park, swimming in the ocean, practicing yoga, or engaging in seated exercises, countless options can be tailored to your individual needs and abilities. By embracing the activities that bring you delight, you transform exercise into a pleasurable experience that you genuinely look forward to.

Let go of preconceived notions and allow yourself to rediscover the joy of movement and play. Exercise is not a one-size-fits-all concept but rather a celebration of what your body can do, no matter the scope of your abilities. It's an opportunity to nurture your physical and mental well-being and challenge yourself in meaningful ways.

No matter where you are on your journey, know that support and inspiration are available to you. Seek out communities, resources, and individuals who can provide guidance and encouragement. Create an inclusive space where you feel empowered to embrace the joy of movement, regardless of your physical capabilities.

So whether you're climbing mountains or engaging in seated exercises, remember that exercise is a universal language that unites us all. It's a celebration of your unique human experience and a testament to the incredible potential that resides within you. Together, let's embark on this adventure, embracing the joy of movement and proving that exercise knows no limitations.

Playtime isn't Just for Kids

Vision into Action: Just like Superman putting on his cape, how will you jump into action? How much time can you commit to daily? Thirty minutes of secret superhero training?

Every day, I'll transform into my exercise superhero self by ____________

____

Over time, I'll level up my training to ____________________

____

The Bare Minimum: How can you guarantee your daily rendezvous with exercise? Maybe keep a pair of sneakers in your car or do five jumping jacks every time you make a cup of coffee?

I'll ensure my daily dose of movement by ____________________

____

Know Your Limits: Just as Superman has Kryptonite, too much exercise can cause your downfall. How will you recognize when to hit the brakes?

I'll know to hit my exercise brakes when ______________________________

____

Celebrate Your Victories: Seeing progress is like finding hidden treasure. How will you track your fitness milestones? Do your jeans fit better? Or perhaps you're not panting after climbing a flight of stairs?

I'll track my fitness treasure map by ______________________________

____

Self-Motivation: We all have those lazy days. What's your secret weapon to battle the "I don't wanna exercise" monster?

I'll Slay the lazy monster by ______________________________________

Barrier Breaker: What potential villains might try to intercept your exercise plans? And how will you overcome them?

The villains that might interfere with my exercise plans are ______________

____

My superhero strategy to overcome these villains is ____________________

____

____

Your Super Squad: Having a trusty sidekick or a loyal league of fitness friends can make your exercise journey more fun and accountable. Who's in your super squad?

My trusty sidekicks in this fitness journey are ________________________

____

When it comes to exercise, remember, there's no one-size-fits-all cape. Your "playouts" should be as unique as your superhero identity, reflecting what you love and what motivates you. So whether you're twirling in a dance class, lunging your way through a game of frisbee, or finding Zen in yoga, embrace the joy of movement. Exercise doesn't have to be a dreaded chore on your to-do list. In fact, when it feels more like play than work, you're more likely to stick with it.

Being physically active is a celebration of what your body can do, not a punishment for what you ate. And it's never too late to start. Remember that even Superman didn't learn to fly overnight. Celebrate your progress, no matter how small it may seem. Each step forward, each rep completed, and each moment you chose activity over inertia is a victory worth celebrating.

And finally, remember that you're not in this alone. Just as every superhero has a trusted sidekick, recruit your own league of extraordinary "playout" pals. Accountability can be a potent motivator; shared experiences always seem to double the fun.

So put on your metaphorical cape, strike your power pose, and embrace the journey of exercise and play. This is your adventure, your story. Make it one for the storybooks!

29

Cultivating Seeds of Transformation

"The mind is like a garden, and thoughts are the seeds.
You can choose to plant flowers or weeds."

- Ralph Waldo Emerson

Unearthing the Power of Seeds

Throughout life's journey, we encounter a bountiful harvest of seeds and golden nuggets. These treasures hold the potential to shape our perspectives, ignite our passions, and inspire meaningful transformations. While the allure of golden nuggets, representing worldly possessions, prizes, and external validation, may captivate our attention, it is the unassuming seeds that hold the true power to create profound change.

In a world driven by the pursuit of material success and external validation, it's easy to become enamored with the glittering allure of golden nuggets. We chase after wealth, fame, and status, believing that they hold the key to our happiness and fulfillment. Yet, these golden nuggets often prove to be fleeting and transient, leaving us longing for more profound meaning and purpose.

On the other hand, the seeds represent the humble offerings of wisdom, love, and genuine human connection. They may appear dull and unremarkable compared to the shiny allure of golden nuggets, but their potential for growth and transformation is immeasurable.

These seeds embody compassion, kindness, empathy, and inner fulfillment.

When we consciously share these seeds with others, we transcend the ego-driven pursuit of golden nuggets. Instead, we invest in the collective growth and well-being of humanity. By cultivating gardens of compassion and understanding, we contribute to a world that values inner richness and genuine human connection over external achievements.

In the tapestry of our lives, we gather seeds from a myriad of expected and unexpected sources. They may be tucked within the pages of a beloved book, hidden within the melodies of a cherished song, or delicately woven into the wisdom shared by those who cross our paths.

These seeds may initially seem small and insignificant, but their potential is boundless.

When we consciously share these seeds with others, we contribute to humanity's collective growth and transformation. We scatter the seeds of self-acceptance, courage, resilience, and empathy with love and intention. We offer them as gifts to uplift and nurture the hearts and minds of those around us. Each seed carries within it the capacity to blossom into extraordinary creations abundant with joy, compassion, and purpose.

However, it is essential to surrender the need to control or force our seeds (beliefs) onto others. Instead, we must cultivate a deep respect for the unique journeys of those we encounter. By sharing seeds without judgment or attachment, we honor the creative genius within each individual, allowing them the freedom to choose how and when to nurture their own garden.

It is crucial to remember that not every seed will take root in the soil of another person's experience. Just as different plants require specific conditions to flourish, each individual possesses unique circumstances, perspectives, and aspirations. Embrace the understanding that the seeds we sow may find fertile ground in unexpected places while others may require different nourishment to grow.

As we embark on this journey of sharing seeds, let us release the need for recognition or credit. Our purpose is not to claim ownership over the growth of others but to be humble witnesses to their blossoming. We find fulfillment in the knowledge that we have contributed to the collective tapestry of human growth and interconnectedness.

Dear wanderer, continue to share your seeds of wisdom, love, and inspiration with the world. Allow them to take flight on the wings of kindness and compassion. Trust in the transformative power of these seeds, knowing that they hold the potential to cultivate a garden of abundance, not only within others but also within yourself. Let us sow the seeds of possibility together and watch our shared gardens flourish into a tapestry of beauty, resilience, and endless growth.

What is the difference between golden nuggets and seeds in life?

The distinction between golden nuggets and seeds is, ____________________

____

How do they impact your growth and fulfillment?

*Golden nuggets impact my growth by*________________________________

____

Seeds impact my growth by ______________________________________

____

Who have you tried to control or force beliefs on?

*Reflecting on past experiences, I realize that I have tried to control or force my beliefs on*____

____

How did that affect your relationships and their receptiveness to your ideas?

*Because I forced beliefs on these people, our relationship has been*__________

____

____

How can you share a seed with them instead? What approaches or methods can you use to offer your perspective or insights without imposing your beliefs on others?

*To share a seed with them, I can approach the situation with empathy and understanding by*____

____

____

What changes will sharing this seed create? How can a tiny seed of wisdom or inspiration lead to significant shifts in someone's life or perspective?

*By sharing this seed, it has the potential to bring about transformative changes such as*____

____

Suppose you don't experience the seed being accepted and planted right away. How will you prevent yourself from becoming discouraged and allow yourself to trust in the process instead of moving backward and becoming forceful or controlling? How can you cultivate patience and faith in the natural growth and unfolding of ideas?

*In such a scenario, I will remind myself to stay patient and trust in the process by*____

____

____

Do you trust yourself to be an observer and not interfere? Why is it important to relinquish control and allow others to nurture the seeds you've shared in their own time and way?

It is essential to trust myself to be an observer without interfering because

____

____

When you do experience the seed take off and grow, how can you show up for them? How can you provide support, encouragement, and guidance to those who have embraced the seeds you've shared?

*To show up for them, I can offer my support and guidance by*____________

____

____

Instead of taking credit for sharing the seed, how can you empower them? How can you celebrate their growth and accomplishments without seeking recognition or validation?

*I can empower them by acknowledging their own efforts and achievements and by*____

____

____

How do you imagine it will feel not to receive any credit? Why is it essential to detach from the need for external recognition and find joy in the act of sharing and witnessing the growth of others?

*Detaching from the need for credit will feel liberating because*____________

____

____

How can you continue cultivating and sharing seeds of wisdom, love, and inspiration with the world? How can you embrace your role as a humble contributor to humanity's collective growth and interconnectedness?

*Moving forward, I can continue to cultivate and share seeds by*___________

____

The Seeds Within—Cultivate Your Inner Garden

"Plant your own gardens and decorate your own soul
instead of waiting for someone to bring you flowers."
-Jorge Luis Borges

As we reflect on the distinction between golden nuggets and seeds, we realize that the true power lies in cultivating your own garden. Just like a skilled gardener tends to their plants with love and care, you too can nurture your own inner world and create a thriving sanctuary within.

Your journey of cultivating your garden begins by recognizing the seeds that reside within you—seeds of wisdom, love, compassion, and personal growth. Through your conscious efforts, you can pluck out the weeds of self-doubt, fear, and negativity and plant the seeds that align with your authentic self.

In this garden of your soul, my friend, you have the power to choose which seeds you want to cultivate and nourish. You can water them with positive affirmations, self-reflection, and personal development practices. Please provide them with the sunlight of self-love, acceptance, and forgiveness. By tending to your inner garden with mindfulness and intention, you create an environment where your seeds can take root and flourish.

As you embark on this beautiful journey of self-cultivation, free yourself from the need for external validation or the pursuit of fleeting golden nuggets. Recognize that true fulfillment and joy come from within as you witness the beauty and abundance that sprouts from your carefully nurtured seeds.

My dear friend, let us embrace the wisdom of cultivating your own garden, knowing that it is a lifelong endeavor. Tend to your inner landscape with patience, perseverance, and self-compassion. Doing so creates a space where your most genuine self can blossom and the flowers of your unique potential bloom in all their vibrant colors.

Imagine that within you lies a beautiful garden, filled with various flowers, each representing various aspects of your being. Some flowers may symbolize your strengths, talents, and passions, while others represent your dreams, aspirations, and potential. Just like a garden, your inner landscape requires your care, attention, and nurturing to thrive.

Take a moment to reflect on your own garden. What flowers are already blooming within you, and what seeds do you wish to plant and cultivate further? Embrace the journey of tending to your inner garden and watch as it flourishes, radiating beauty and becoming a true reflection of your authentic self.

Let's dig a little deeper and explore the seeds within you. What good seeds do you have within you that are already growing?

*The good seeds within me are*____

____

Next, acknowledge the weed seeds that may be present within you. Are they fear, sadness, anxiety, depression, or trauma?

*The weeds I see inside me are*____________________________________

____

Dig deep and find the roots of these weeds. What caused them to grow, and where did they come from?

*The root causes of my weeds are from*____________________________

____

____

As you continue to tend to your garden, it's important to pluck out these weeds so they don't continue hindering your growth. What steps will you take to remove and prevent these weeds from causing further harm?

*The steps I will take to remove these weeds from my life are*______________

____

____

____

Imagine how it will feel when you have successfully weeded your inner garden, your personal sanctuary.

*After pulling the weeds, my inner sanctuary will feel*___________________

____

To ensure the ongoing health and vitality of your inner garden, how will you attend to and nourish it daily?

*I will nourish my garden daily by*________________________________

____

____

Now, take a moment to envision your life when all the weeds have been plucked out of your mind, and your inner sanctuary truly becomes a place of peace, joy, and abundance. How will this transformation impact your relationships, self-confidence, and overall life experience?

*Having a beautiful inner sanctuary within me will allow life to be*________

____

____

____

As we come to the end of this chapter, let us take a moment to reflect on the profound wisdom and insights we have gathered. We have explored the distinction between golden nuggets and seeds, realizing that the true power lies in cultivating our own garden. We have recognized the importance of nurturing the seeds of wisdom, love, compassion, and personal growth within ourselves.

Just like a skilled gardener tends to their plants with love and care, we too have the ability to tend to our inner world and create a thriving sanctuary within. We have learned that cultivating our garden begins with self-awareness and the willingness to uproot the weeds of self-doubt, fear, and negativity. Through conscious effort and nurturing, we can sow the seeds of positivity, self-love, and personal development.

As we embark on the journey of cultivating our own garden, we free ourselves from the need for external validation or the pursuit of fleeting golden nuggets. We realize that true fulfillment and joy come from within as we witness the beauty and abundance that sprouts from our carefully nurtured seeds.

The journey of tending to your inner garden is a lifelong endeavor. It requires patience, perseverance, and self-compassion. You may encounter setbacks along the way, but your garden will continue to flourish through mindful attention and intentional nurturing.

My dear friend, as you reflect on your own garden, remember that you have the power to shape and transform it. Take the time to identify the good seeds already blooming within you and celebrate their presence. Be honest about the weed seeds that may be hindering your growth and commit to plucking them out with love and understanding.

Embrace the journey of tending to your inner garden, for it is in this sacred space that you will find inner peace, joy, and freedom. Nurture your garden daily with mindfulness, self-care, and personal growth practices. Cultivate an environment where your seeds can take root and blossom to their full potential.

As we move forward, let us carry the wisdom of cultivating our garden. Let us continue to tend to our inner landscape, knowing that with each passing day, we can nurture and cultivate a rich tapestry of experiences, wisdom, and self-discovery.

May your garden be abundant with vibrant flowers of personal growth, fulfillment, and authenticity. May you find solace, inspiration, and joy in the beauty of your cultivated sanctuary.

30

Embracing the Flow of Existence

"Row, row, row your boat, gently down the stream.
Merrily, merrily, merrily, life is but a dream."

-Unknown

Discovering Life's Harmony

As we reach the concluding chapter of this remarkable journey, let us dive deeper into the profound wisdom hidden within the simple verses of "Row, Row, Your Boat." This timeless nursery rhyme holds within it a powerful message that resonates throughout our lives, inviting us to embrace the essence of our existence.

Row, row ...

You will need to row your boat. Life is not a passive experience; it requires our active participation. Just as a boat needs the gentle strokes of an oar to move downstream, our lives demand effort and determination. We must row forward, embracing the challenges and obstacles that come our way. Remember that the direction of your journey is in your hands. With each row, you propel yourself forward, navigating the ebb and flow of life's currents.

Row your boat.

Your boat represents your unique existence, your body, and your life's purpose. It is a vessel that carries your hopes, dreams, and aspirations. Avoid the temptation to row someone else's boat, for their journey is not yours to navigate. Find the courage to chart your own course, following the inner compass guiding you toward your destination. Your boat, your life, your choices. Trust in your inner wisdom and sail towards fulfilling your dreams.

Gently down the stream.

Life flows with a natural rhythm, an ever-changing current that carries us forward. It is not about forcefully fighting against the current but rather surrendering to its gentle embrace. When we navigate with grace and ease, we align ourselves with the divine flow of existence. Embrace the beauty of surrender and allow life to unfold in its own perfect timing. Trust that the stream knows the way, and you will be guided toward the experiences and opportunities that align with your highest good.

Merrily merrily, merrily, merrily.

Embrace a life filled with joy and merriment. Allow laughter to be your soundtrack and happiness your constant companion. Follow your passions, listen to the whispers of your heart, and live in alignment with your true purpose. As you do so, the journey becomes a delightful dance, and every step becomes an expression of your authentic self. Find joy in the simple pleasures, celebrate your successes, and savor each precious moment along the way.

Life is but a dream.

Pause for a moment and contemplate the profound nature of existence. Life is not merely a series of events but a grand illusion, a dream from which we awaken. We are spiritual beings temporarily inhabiting physical bodies, experiencing the vastness of creation. Please recognize that the stories we create in our minds shape our perception of reality. Through higher awareness and expanded consciousness, we can awaken from the dream and discover the limitless potential that lies within. Embrace the beauty of life's dreamlike nature and explore the infinite possibilities that unfold before you.

Now, my dear friend, I invite you to embark on a transformative exercise—a walking meditation that mirrors the essence of "Row, Row, Your Boat." Take each step with mindfulness, allowing your feet to guide you without an agenda or destination. Immerse yourself in the present moment, using all your senses to embrace the path before you. As you wander, reflect on each section of the rhyme, and uncover the more profound insights they hold.

In this moment of reflection, let go of the illusion of control and surrender to the flow of existence. Embrace the adventure that life offers, knowing that you have the power to shape your experience. Nurture your dreams, row your boat with intention, and allow the melody of merriment to accompany you on this extraordinary journey. Trust in the beauty of life's unfolding and savor every moment with a grateful heart.

Remember, my friend, that life is but a dream. Awake now, and live each moment with purpose, passion, and profound gratitude.

Unlock the Secrets of Your Soul, Journal Your Journey of Self-Discovery

Taking the time to journal about your experience can deepen your reflection and help you gain further insights. It lets you capture your thoughts, emotions, and observations, providing a record of your journey and personal growth. Journaling can be a powerful tool for self-discovery and self-expression.

Find a quiet and comfortable space where you can sit with your journal. Take a few deep breaths to center yourself and bring your attention to the present moment. Then, using the prompts below, begin to write about your walking meditation experience:

1. Describe the sensations you felt during the walking meditation. How did it feel to be fully present and connected to your surroundings?
2. Reflect on any insights or realizations that came to you during the meditation. Did you notice any patterns or recurring thoughts? What messages or guidance did you receive?
3. Explore how the "Row, Row, Your Boat" concept resonates with your life journey. What does it mean to you to row your own boat and go with the flow? How can you apply this wisdom to your current life circumstances?
4. Consider the significance of gently rowing your boat and embracing the flow. How does this relate to self-compassion, self-care, and finding balance in your life?
5. Write about any challenges or obstacles you encountered during the meditation and how you navigated through them. What lessons did you learn from these experiences?
6. Finally, express gratitude or appreciation for the insights and moments of clarity you gained during the walking meditation. What are you grateful for in your life right now?

Journaling is a powerful tool that allows you to capture the essence of your experiences, thoughts, and emotions. It provides a window into your soul, a safe space to explore the depths of your being. As you embark on this walking meditation journey, I encourage you to continue journaling throughout your life's journey, for it is in the act of writing that we uncover the hidden treasures within us.

Journaling is a mere record-keeping activity and a profound act of self-reflection and self-expression. It is a conversation between you and your inner voice, a dialogue that unravels the mysteries of your thoughts and feelings. By putting pen to paper, you give voice to the whispers of your soul and provide a tangible form to the intangible.

The importance of journaling cannot be overstated. It is a companion that accompanies you on your quest, a witness to your growth, and a source of solace in times of turmoil. It captures the nuances of your experiences, the lessons learned, and the dreams woven within your heart. It serves as a compass, guiding you back to your most authentic self when you feel lost or uncertain.

In the pages of your journal, you will find a sanctuary where you can freely express yourself, unburden your heart, and find solace in the written word. It is a sacred space where you can reflect on the beauty of life, explore your aspirations, and delve into the depths of your soul.

My dear friend, keep your journal close as you embark on this walking meditation experience and beyond. Let it be your confidant, sounding board, and guiding light. Fill its pages with your dreams, insights, and reflections, and watch as the words on the paper become a testament to your growth, resilience, and the beauty of your unique journey.

Remember that the journey of life is best traversed with a pen in hand, ready to capture the miracles and lessons that unfold along the way. May your journal be a faithful companion throughout the adventure, a source of inspiration, and a treasured keepsake of your ever-evolving story.

CONCLUSION

Living the Adventure of You

Allow the wisdom and insights gained from "Row, Row, Your Boat" to guide you as you continue on your adventure of life. Just as each step in the meditation allowed you to be fully present and embrace the flow of the path, every moment in your journey is an opportunity for growth, self-discovery, and transformation.

As you walk through the various landscapes and terrains that life presents, remember to stay mindful and open to the experiences that come your way. Allow yourself to be guided by intuition, curiosity, and a sense of wonder. Embrace the twists and turns, the uphill climbs, and the gentle descents, for they are all part of the rich tapestry of your unique adventure.

Be attentive to the signs and synchronicities that appear along your path, guiding you toward new opportunities, connections, and revelations. Listen to the whispers of your heart, as it knows the way to your deepest desires and authentic self. Trust in the guidance of the universe, for it conspires in mysterious ways to support your growth and fulfillment.

During moments of uncertainty or challenge, remember that you have the power to choose how you respond. Gently guide your thoughts back to awareness whenever they stray into worry or doubt. Cultivate a mindset of resilience, gratitude, and self-belief, knowing that each step forward is a testament to your inner strength and courage.

On your journey of life's adventure, let joy be your compass and love be your guiding star. Find delight in the simple pleasures, celebrate your accomplishments, and share kindness and compassion with fellow travelers along the way. Embrace the beauty of the journey, for it is in the unfolding moments that you discover the depths of your being and the magic of existence.

My dear friend, savor the gift of being alive with each step you take. Embrace the wonder of this ever-changing, dreamlike existence. Allow the lessons and inspiration gathered throughout this journey to fuel your growth, resilience, and inner wisdom. Remember that life is a grand adventure, and you have the power to create a story that is uniquely yours.

As you continue walking your own adventure of life, may your heart be filled with gratitude, your spirit be ignited with passion, and your path be adorned with love and fulfillment. Keep moving forward, for infinite wonders are awaiting your discovery. Embrace the adventure, and let your footsteps leave an indelible mark on the tapestry of existence.

The adventure awaits, my friend. Walk on, and may every step be a testament to the extraordinary journey of your soul. Keep delving into the depths; eventually, you may find yourself back where you began. Yet, on this voyage, you shall behold the familiar with fresh eyes, understanding it anew for the first time.

"Lives of great men all remind us
We can make our lives sublime,
And, departing, leave behind us
Footprints on the sands of time."

-Henry Wadsworth Longfellow

Printed in the United States
by Baker & Taylor Publisher Services